PSYCHOSEXUAL DISORDERS
A REVIEW

Publication Number 1027

AMERICAN LECTURE SERIES®

A Monograph in

The BANNERSTONE DIVISION *of*
AMERICAN LECTURES IN LIVING CHEMISTRY

Edited by

I. NEWTON KUGELMASS, M.D., Ph.D., Sc.D.
Consultant to the Department of Health and Hospitals
New York, New York

PSYCHOSEXUAL DISORDERS
A REVIEW

By

M.T. HASLAM, M.A., M.D., M.R.C.P., M.R.C. Psych., D.M.J.

Consultant Psychiatrist
Clifton Hospital
York, England

With a Foreword by

Martin Cole, Ph.D.

Department of Biological Sciences
University of Aston
Birmingham, England
Institute for Sex Education and Research
Moseley
Birmingham, England

CHARLES C THOMAS • PUBLISHER
Springfield • Illinois • U.S.A.

Published and Distributed Throughout the World by
CHARLES C THOMAS • PUBLISHER
BANNERSTONE HOUSE
301-327 East Lawrence Avenue, Springfield, Illinois, U.S.A.

© *1979, by* CHARLES C THOMAS • PUBLISHER
ISBN 0-398-03903-8
Library of Congress Catalog Card Number: 79-41

With THOMAS BOOKS *careful attention is given to all details of
manufacturing and design. It is the Publisher's desire to present
books that are satisfactory as to their physical qualities and artistic
possibilities and appropriate for their particular use.* THOMAS
BOOKS *will be true to those laws of quality that assure a good
name and good will.*

Printed in the United States of America
N-11

Library of Congress Cataloging in Publication Data

Haslam, Michael Trevor.
    Psychosexual disorders.

    (American lecture series ; publication no. 1027)
    Bibliography: p.
    Includes index.
    1. Sexual disorders. 2. Sexual deviation. I. Title. [DNLM: 1. Sex-
ual deviation. 2. Sexual disorders. WM611 H325p]
RC556.H39   616.6   79-41
ISBN 0-398-03903-8

To Maureen

FOREWORD

SEX THERAPY is a new subject: It is essentially interdisciplinary, and those involved require the skills of many distinct specialties — academic, clinical and paramedical. No therapist can manage on his own; he requires the help and support of a team if he is to provide his patient with realistic treatment.

This impressive review of psychosexual disorders by Michael Haslam is therefore very welcome. It performs that necessary role of integrating up-to-date information from the many disciplines involved in the treatment of sex disorders and sexual variations. The information is presented in an attractively written style which makes it compulsive reading for anyone who is involved either intimately or peripherally in the subject.

The author's approach is based upon fact and the scientific method, yet he has also fairly represented a wide range of opinion, particularly in his discussion of the aetiology of sex deviations.

There has been a rash of new books on this subject, some good and others not, the latter often propagating untested ideas and secondhand opinions. In this review, the author has taken an independent, objective and critical look at the literature and added his personal touch — all of which should enable a wide range of readers to acquaint themselves with recent developments in our understanding of the aetiology and therapy of psychosexual disorders. Of particular value is the way the author has dealt with the more "difficult" area of sex deviation. Often in the past, these behaviours have been neglected by the sex therapist. Michael Haslam has presented a very balanced account emphasising, where appropriate, that often it is societal values that are at fault, without disregarding the role of therapy when it is called for.

The author is a psychiatrist and is well qualified to write about psychosexual disorders. He presents the results of his own work and experience in the wider context of a thorough review of the literature, writing not only as a scientist and clinician, but also as one with an undeniable humanity, understanding and sympathy for those who have the misfortune to suffer from one or other form of sexual handicap.

MARTIN COLE, PH.D.

PREFACE

THIS IS A BOOK for the specialist and for those interested in exploring in depth the history and practice of sexology. Set out in review form, an extensive bibliography of 130 references allows wide further reading on particular topics beyond those which are extensively quoted in the manuscript.

Sexual problems fall readily into two groups: the partnership problems which may be found in heterosexual couple activity, and the anomalies of sexual behaviour or paraphilias, which include homosexuality, transvestism and deviancies.

The book divides into three parts. The first is an extensive review of the literature in historical perspective including reference to classical Indian, Arabic and Chinese writings. The second part covers the main categories of partnership dysfunctions, erective and arousal failures, ejaculatory disturbances and vaginismus. A chapter is also devoted to a neglected section of sexual problems, namely the handicapped. The third part is devoted to the paraphilias, with a chapter on the medico-legal problems which can arise.

This is the author's second work devoted to sexual problems; he has already published a successful work on sexual disorders for the general practitioner or counsellor, designed for simpler reading and as a rule-of-thumb guide to therapy of interest to the general reader (*Sexual Disorders,* London, Pitman, 1978). This second work is geared to a more specialized readership and thus complements rather than replaces the first.

INTRODUCTION

IN RECENT YEARS there has been an increasing awareness of the
extent of the problem posed, in terms of human unhappiness
and professional time, by disorders of sexual function. There had
been, until Kinsey's publications, little awareness indeed of even
the range of normal sexual function, and it was perhaps not until
Masters and Johnson pioneered the study of the physiology of
sexual response that professional interest began to be evoked.

Until this time psychosexual problems had either been left
untreated, a matter of taboo and prejudice, or for the wealthy,
an occasion for the psycho-analyst's couch. It was freely recognized, however, that partnership problems typified by impotence
and frigidity as well as disorders of sexual identity such as homosexuality were little modified by the "talking cure."

Masters and Johnson's second book, which discussed their
treatment programme for what they termed *human sexual inadequacies,* showed that behavioural methods had considerably more
to offer. This pioneering work resulted in increased hope for
sufferers and increased awareness of the existence of such problems by professionals who were engaged in therapy. As a result
many groups have sprung up to counsel in this field, some orthodox and reputable, some fringe and bordering on the charlatan.

At the same time there has developed in the last few years the
ability to identify, with increasing accuracy, cases where biochemical or hormonal disturbances have played a major part in
the aetiology of such dysfunctions. In addition, the part which
drugs given to the patient in the treatment of some other problem can play in the iatrogenic cause of sexual dysfunctions has
been recognized. A not inconsiderable proportion of cases which
would previously have been assumed to be totally psychological
in origin and treated therefore with psychotherapeutic techniques

have now been able to be recognized as having an organic component.

Psychosexual disorders can be divided conveniently into two main groupings. The first of these are what Masters and Johnson have called human sexual inadequacies, a rather unfortunate phrase with which to label one's clients. Perhaps *sexual partnership problems* would be better, though of course not all sufferers have a current partner. They include four main groups of conditions commonly known as impotence, frigidity, premature ejaculation and vaginismus. Ejaculatory failure is also occasionally found.

The terms *impotency* and *frigidity* are in the author's view best avoided. They are descriptively too vague and have come into general usage by the public almost as terms of abuse. The frigid lady is one who will not go to bed when the man wants her to. It is better to classify these conditions as arousal or erective incompetence in the first case and orgasmic incompetence in the other. Both these conditions can occur in the male or the female, and there are important differences in the aetiology in many cases. Such conditions may be primary or secondary. That is to say, they may have existed from the beginning of the individual's sexual life or may have been encountered more recently. This has important diagnostic significance. The conditions may be partial or total. Thus at the time of history taking, the orgasmic or erective failure may be complete and occur on every occasion that sex play is initiated, or it may in contrast occur on some occasions with a particular partner and not other occasions, or if more than one partner is involved, it may occur with one partner and not with the other partner.

At the Clinic for Psycho-Sexual Disorders in York, England, a survey of 100 consecutive referrals showed that some 80 percent fell into this category of partnership dysfunctions (Haslam, 1975).

The second group of psychosexual disorders embraces those conditions where the sexual response is distorted from the hypothetical heterosexual norm. Again, there is no one word in common parlance to cover the various conditions which would be included. Deviancy is unsatisfactory in that a considerable body of opinion would deny that homosexuality is in itself a pattern of deviant response, but rather that it is a normal minority variant of no more medical or psychiatric significance than might be ginger hair. Furthermore, the majority of transvestites might accept that they had a distortion of gender orientation but would not be happy to be classed as sexually deviant, as they would not see their condition as basically a sexual problem.

This group will be, for want of a better word, classified as *sexual behavioural anomalies*. It will include problems arising from homosexual orientation, problems arising from gender identity distortions as in transvestism and transsexualism, and patterns of deviant sexual response which can be considered under four sub-groups, namely paedophilia, fetishism, sadomasochism and exhibitionism-voyeurism. One could, of course, expand on this list and include rarities or fringe sexual activities. Indeed it might be logical to include masturbation as a sexual deviancy on the basis that it is not designed towards the practice of the hypothetical heterosexual norm. On the other hand, since it is an almost universal practise at some stage in an individual's life, which is more than can be said for heterosexual intercourse, one might argue that this is the normal and heterosexual intercourse deviant!

These problems are semantic. In practice some 20 percent of referrals come from these groups and the doctor must be seen as a counsellor and adviser rather than applying any preconceived stereotypes of his own which might result in distorted and biased advice.

In this monograph we shall look firstly at the historical perspective of psychosexual disorders. We shall consider concepts of causation with particular reference to more recent ideas on some biological and biochemical aspects and shall outline present trends in therapy and management of these cases, both in those conditions where a partnership problem is manifest and in those where a distortion of sexual orientation has taken place.

ACKNOWLEDGMENTS

I WOULD LIKE to acknowledge the help given by my colleagues in the York Psychosexual Clinic and to the other authors quoted in this manuscript. I would like to thank Miss Hudson and Miss Luxton for the secretarial help given in the preparation of the book, and my wife, Shirley, for help in the proofreading. I would especially wish to acknowledge the cooperation of my artists, Cliff and Wendy Meadway of Hailsham, who prepared the drawings.

M.T.H.

CONTENTS

PSYCHOSEXUAL DISORDERS
A REVIEW

Section I

CLASSIFICATION AND HISTORICAL REVIEW

Chapter 1

CLASSIFICATION

In cupid's school
Who e'er would take degree
Must learn his rudiments
By reading me.

OVID

THE STUDY OF PSYCHOSEXUAL disorders falls naturally into two basic sub-divisions, the first where there is a disturbance of performance of the sexual act, primarily the result of a partnership problem and relating to difficulties experienced between the couple. The second is where sexual activity is different from the so-called heterosexual norm, which we call for want of a better term sexual behavioural anomalies.

This latter category is sometimes known as sexual perversion or deviance and has traditionally been subdivided by a descriptive terminology relating to the particular distortion practised. While this may be useful in purely descriptive terms, it is an artificial division, the boundaries of which are often fluid. Indeed, the question of perversion covers a multitude of sins and relates principally to the contemporary morality of the society involved.

The classification followed in the *Index Medicus* shows two primary groups concerned with psychosexual disorders: one entitled "Sex Disorders (psychological in nature general term)"; and the other "Sex Deviation (general term includes coprophilia, exhibitionism, fetishism, paedophilia and voyeurism)." The headings are arranged in hierarchies within each subject. Concepts are indexed under the most specific heading available. Concepts not covered by an unique heading are covered by the next most

5

general term, and the terms are arranged in alphabetical order, citations listed under each term being arranged in groups by the use of sub-headings.

In addition to the general heading of sex disorders and included under this group are dyspareunia, frigidity and impotence, each given a separate classification; under sex deviation there are in addition headings specified for homosexuality, incest, masochism, masturbation, sadism, transsexualism and transvestism.

This type of classification may be useful in terms of abstracting articles for research, but it leaves out some problems and is over-inclusive of others. For example, community surveys performed by Kinsey have shown that some practises, while strictly deviant by some definitions, are sufficiently widely practised at some phases of development (for example masturbation in adolescence) as to be considered a normal facet of human behaviour. Similarly, incest, although prohibited by law in many countries, would nevertheless not fall into the category of deviation by some definitions since it is a normal heterosexual act between a male and a female.

Masters and Johnson's scholarly works on the physiology of human sexual response and on what they call human sexual inadequacy classify the first group, namely disturbances of performance of the sexual act, into the following subdivisions: (1) premature ejaculation, (2) ejaculatory incompetence, (3) primary and secondary impotence, (4) orgasmic dysfunction and (5) vaginismus. Again, there is some overlap in these conditions, and the distinction between orgasmic disorders in the male and in the female tends to emphasize the differences rather than similarities. For practical purposes, however, the distinction may be useful.

Attempts in recent times to classify sexual deviance date back to Ulrich in the mid-nineteenth century who sub-divided conditions into "urnings" and "dionings." Most schools of thought since this time have considered the majority of deviations to be acquired but have included a congenital group. Thus Krafft-Ebing in his work *Psychopathia Sexualis* conceded that some have a circumscribed perversion whilst in others the whole personality is involved. Kinsey introduced a useful concept of innate human bisexuality and considered that every individual could be rated on a six-point scale from exclusively heterosexual to exclusively homosexual. He found, however, that the majority of individuals had some traits which could be interpreted as homo-erotic and pointed out that it was in the nature of the human frame that this might be expected to be so.

An interesting classification was elaborated by P. D. Scott in 1970 and by other workers such as D. J. West and A. Store. The concept was that the degree of partner interaction could be subdivided into (1) those who were unable to make a personal relationship at all, (2) those unable to make a co-operative relationship, (3) those requiring exceptional circumstances or conditions for a partner relationship to be initiated, and (4) those who could make a relationship but were unable to achieve a complete and satisfying normal sexual union. This seems a rational method of grouping psychosexual problems in terms of the maturity of the social relationship which the individual can achieve. It must be recognized, however, that deviant behaviour and psychosexual disorders may occur in exceptional personality structures, and this may colour the nature of the sexual experience. Indeed, it may influence research in terms of the type of individual who can be contacted and who may attend for treatment. Thus the personality structure of the subject could be considered under such headings as (1) adolescents and mentally immature adults who are undecided in their role, (2) severely damaged personalities such as the paranoid or anti-social types, (3) relatively intact personalities who enjoy their perversion and who can be said to be experimenting in a wider form of self-expression, and (4) individuals whose problems coexist with or are released by serious psychiatric illness such as schizophrenia or dementia.

The concepts enumerated above have general relevance in terms of possible factors involved in aetiology. These can be considered as (1) inherited, (2) secondary to psychiatric illness, or (3) acquired by conditioning. This latter may relate to critical stages in development along the lines of the concept of imprinting or might relate to indirect social factors of dominance and submission within the peer group. Equally, it could be sub-cultural and the result of prohibitions, particularly of a religious character, or from entrenched problems in the individual which relate to fear of close contact with the opposite sex.

Chapter 2

HISTORICAL REVIEW

THAT MAN MUST apprentice himself to the art of satisfactory love-making has been known since earliest literary times and is well summed up in the words of the playwright W.S. Gilbert who quotes:

A man who would woo a fair maid
Must apprentice himself to the trade
And practise all day
In methodical way
How to flatter, cajole and persuade.

In the literature of all countries, there is to be found a certain number of works treating specifically the subject of love-making. The standard work on love in Sanskrit literature is *The Kama Sutra* or *Aphorisms of Love* by Vatsyayana. This book is impossible to date accurately but must have been written sometime between the first and sixth centuries. The book gives in detail various methods which may be employed in intercourse and related matters. It is an interesting social study of the customs of the time, and although problems of deviant behaviour are not specifically considered, comment is made upon those customs acceptable in society which perhaps in other cultures and other times might be considered as perverse. This clearly makes the point that to describe a sexual activity as deviant can only be valid in the culture and decade to which it is applied.

In Part 6 of *The Kama Sutra,* a number of chapters are devoted to a discussion on courtesans and prostitutes and how the individual should behave towards them. Fellatio is described in

9

Part 2, Chapter 9 as the *auparishtaka* or mouth congress. In this culture to perform such acts between married partners was considered indecent, but the practise was legitimate when practised by eunuchs or courtesans.

The book also describes legitimate homosexuality and evidence of transvestism. Thus "eunuchs disguised as females may imitate their dress, speech, gestures, tenderness, timidity, simplicity, softness and bashfulness. The acts that are done on the middle parts of women are done in the mouths of these eunuchs and this is known as auparishtaka. Such eunuchs derive their imaginable pleasure and their livelihood from this type of congress and lead the life of a courtesan. Eunuchs disguised as males keep their desires secret and when they wish to do anything they lead the lives of shampooers. Under the pretence of shampooing an eunuch of this kind may embrace and draw himself towards the thighs of the man whom he is shampooing and after this he touches the joints of his thighs and if he finds the lingam of the man to be erect he presses it with his hands and after knowing his intention the eunuch may proceed."

The authors, however, are of the opinion that "auparishtaka is the work of a dog and not a man because it is a low practice and opposed to the orders of the Holy writ, because the man himself suffers by bringing his lingam into contact with the mouths of eunuchs and women." Vatsyayana says that the orders of the holy writ do not affect those who resort to courtesans, and the law prohibits the practise of the auparishtaka with married women only.

Sexual inadequacy is briefly touched upon in Part 7 where advice is given on various medicaments for increasing sexual vigour, and an account is given of sexual aids which could be used in connection with or in place of the penis.

Classical Arabic literature also contains books giving advice on the sexual arts, the best known being that of *The Perfumed Garden* by Sheikh Nefzauoni and translated, as was *The Kama Sutra,* by Sir Richard Burton. This work was written at the beginning of the sixth century, at about the year 925 of the Hegira, and emanated from Tunis. This book again gives advice on many items concerning sexual practice. Thus "do not mount upon a woman fasting or immediately before making a meal or else you will have pains in your back. You will lose your vigour and your eyesight will get weaker." Or again "do not leave your member in the vulva after ejaculation as this might cause gravel or softening of the vertebral column." "Avoid washing your member after the copulation as this may cause canker. As to coition with old women it acts like a fatal poison and it has been said do not rummage old women were they as rich as Karoun."

Chapter 14, however, deals with the treatment of sterility in women, suggesting that this may be due to obstruction in the uterus, defective sperm in the male or organic malformations.

Chapter 16 enters into a discussion on the causes of impotence in the male. Here are described hypospadias and premature ejaculation, though the principal cause is considered to be due to shortness of the virile member. The remedy for this latter is considered to be the consumption of honey, ginger and other spices. Psychogenic impotence is, however, also described in Chapter 17: "It will happen for instance that a man with his verge in erection will find it getting flaccid just when he is on the point of introducing it between the thighs of the woman. He thinks this is impotence while it is simply the result of an exaggerated respect for the woman or maybe of a misplaced bashfulness or maybe because he has observed something disagreeable on account of an unpleasant odour. Finally, owing to a feeling of jealousy inspired by the reflection that the woman is no longer a virgin and has served the pleasures of other men."

These observations made over a thousand years ago could well have come from Masters and Johnson's recent treatise.

The Chinese have one of the world's greatest and longest artistic traditions; its treasures have been collected and imitated for centuries in the West. The precepts of Taoism give a direct approach to the strange universe of fluid energies which were manipulated by its sexual and yogic practises. The great Chinese text devoted to Taoism, especially the *Tao-te-Ching* and the *Chuang-Tzu,* are collections of sayings and allegories which point to its meaning from different directions.

Taoism flourished at different times in various parts of China, generated many variant doctrines and produced a vast literature. The *Tao-Tsing* is a Ming-printed collection of these dated A.D. 1445 and contains 1,464 individual works. Certainly, however, the philosophies go back at least to the Sung dynasty of A.D. 960 to 1279 and all share a common attitude to the world and to art.

The Chinese have always taken it very much for granted that sex has a central place in life. Although Confucians may have disapproved of it being much discussed in public, in private, relations between the sexes were a vital concern. Polygamy was normal at that time and had become institutionalized as a status symbol wherein special conditions in the household prevailed. One man was obliged to satisfy sexually many women without reducing himself to a state of exhaustion. Men, therefore, had to learn a large number of erotic techniques, the fundamental skill being for the man to be able to bring several women to orgasm without experiencing orgasm himself. These were the outward signs of Taoist belief which was shaped by the theory of Yin and Yang. The Taoist idea was that sexual essences were secreted by men and women when they became sexually aroused; these essences were material forms of energies that in men were called yang and in women yin. By orgasm the energies were released out of the body and could be absorbed by the partner of the opposite sex through their sexual organs. Each man or woman needed to receive generous doses of the energy of the opposite sex to travel far along the road to self-cultivation. This gave an ambiguity to Chinese sexual life, and erotic skills became particularly important. Many handbooks were written giving careful instruction as to how often, what times of the day and which seasons of the year people of different ages should enjoy sex. Instructions are given as to how the act should be performed so as to give the greatest benefit to all the participants. Preliminary amorous play stimulated the yang and yin and secretions began to flow. Six styles of penetration were described. During intercourse men and women bring each other to the highest pitch of excitement and tension using nine styles of movement and postures whose names in themselves were vivid poetical metaphors such as "bamboos near the altar, reversed flying duck and cat and mouse in one hole." Alternating deep and shallow thrusts might follow the rhythm of different movements, and again these were given special names. Movements "should be varied and full of invention suiting the moods and needs of both partners from moment to moment. They were called by such names as prying open an oyster to reach the pearl, sparrow pecking rich grains and brave soldier flailing right and left to break the enemy ranks."

The male and female sexual organs had names whose imagery formed part of the secret language of Taoism and is portrayed in much of their art. The male was "the red bird, the jade stalk, the coral stem and so on." The female was referred to as "the peach, the open peony blossom, the vermilion gate, the golden lotus, etc." Intercourse was referred to as "the bursting of the clouds and the rain." Plum blossom, which is a favorite subject in Taoist art, was actually a name given for sexual pleasure.

Rawson and Legeza state: "Sex carried out so intensively and with such poetic care enormously enhances the yang in men and the yin in women. Orgasm releases the most potent essences and after orgasm these essences need to be carefully absorbed and skilled and generous lovers will make a complete exchange." Cinnaba, a crystalline stone ground up and used as a red pigment in painting, was in Taoist symbolism the nuclear energy of the joined yang and yin. Since the stone contains a sulphide of mercury, its use led to the deaths of many Taoists, even including some Chinese emperors who after swallowing repeated doses of it died of mercury poisoning.

Classical Roman literature owes much of its works on the art of love to the poet Ovid who wrote *The Art of Love* and *The Remedy Of Love* a few years before his exile. In the introduction to the English translation of these works published in London in 1782, it is stated that "this poet wrote these books a few years before his exile under colour of which the decree of the Senate for his banishment was procured, though they certainly were not the cause of it, and indeed could not reasonably be so unless Ovid wrote them in favour of Augustus' grand-daughter whom he visited with a little too much familiarity and did it to please her. For she no more than her mother, Aggripa's wife, was not so modest as persons of quality and high condition ought to be, as well as for their own glory as for the example to others."

European literature of more recent times has not been lacking in advice to the would-be wooer. *Psychopathia Sexualis* by Richard von Krafft-Ebing, a textbook published in German in 1886 is probably, however, the first orthodox medical textbook on psychosexual disorders as such. Krafft-Ebing, in his introduction to the first edition, states "the object of this treatise is to record the various psychological manifestations of sexual life in men and to trace how they are conditioned by regular laws." This book was the subject of a recent review by Johnson (Johnson, 1973) in the *British Journal of Psychiatry*.

Krafft-Ebing produced a classification of sexual disorders distinguishing between perversion, which he felt was a disease, and acts which resulted from vice or depravity, which he distinguished as perversity. He comments that perversions were frequently associated with brain damage and suggested a possible localization in the brain in relationship to the olfactory centres because of the frequency with which sexual excitement was associated with olfactory stimuli. Krafft-Ebing considered that the content of a perversion was determined by the quality of sexual experience to which the individual had been exposed during development; he expressed this factor in terms of associationism. Krafft-Ebing also gave the first clinical descriptions of *sadism* and *masochism*, terms which he derived from the writings of De Sade and Sacher-Masoch (Deleuze, 1971). He also produced classical descriptions of fetishism and discussed the problem of transvestism.

It was not until 1905, some two years after the death of Krafft-Ebing, that Freud wrote his three essays on sexuality and emphasized how common fetishistic objects might have erotic feeling displaced onto them. These he considered to be phallic equivalents, reassuring the fetishist against castration anxiety.

Bullough (1976), in his book *Sexual Variance in Society and History*, discusses the Jewish contribution to sexuality and the sources of Western attitudes. In Part 2 he elaborates the European inheritance through the contribution of the Greeks and Roman mythology. He also discusses sexual attitudes in the religious creeds of Islam and early Christianity and in the civilisation of Byzantium.

A more recent work by Crown (1976) on psychosexual problems brings up to date present attitudes and aspects relating to sexual minorities and psychosexual problems in a religious setting.

Although attention has been given over some fifteen centuries to the art of the lover and to the problems created by inadequacy of sexual performance, it is only in relatively recent years that serious attention has been turned to problems associated with deviation. Indeed, the term *homosexuality* has itself only been invoked within the last century. Some specific perversions have, however, been described in some of the older literature, and perhaps not surprisingly in view of its widespread occurrence in society, homosexuality has featured widely in such writings.

Thus, Sir Richard Burton in his terminal essay to the translation of *The Arabian Nights* (Burton, 1885), instances the condition as "endemic in various parts of the world including the Mediterranean, the Far East and the Pacific Island," quoting from such various sources as *Male Brothels in the Middle East, Activities in French Society under the Second Empire, The Romantic Male Love of Classical Greece,* and *The Debauchers of the Caesars.*

References to homosexuality occur in Old Testament writings, where the practise was both indulged in and condemned. Some homosexual acts have ritualistic significance for alien religions. Genesis Chapter 19 describes the story of the men of Sodom who stormed the house where Lot was living, demanding "where are the men which came into thee this night? Bring them out to us that we may know them." Further examples occur in Judges 19, I Samuel 20, Samuel 1, and Ruth 1.

Male homosexual sentiment was common to the structure of Greek society where it was idealized as the highest and noblest of passions (Licht, 1926). In the Doric states it was the usual practice for an older man to take under his wing some favourite youth and act as his special friend and counsellor. A man failed in his duty if he did not do so and a youth felt disgraced if he failed to win such friendship. The Spartan and Theban armies were organized on a similar theory, the latter consisting of pairs of such lovers fighting side by side. Indiscriminate infatuations, however, were not encouraged, as is seen by the discrediting of Socrates. Moreover, the cult of effeminacy in young men and the buying and selling of sexual favours were strongly disapproved of, and the penal code of ancient Athens included various provisions against homosexual abuses, some of which dated back to the laws of Solomon.

Solomon's enactments in the sixth century B.C. made relations between adult male citizens permitted, but all civil rights were removed from any Athenian citizen who prostituted his body for money, and the legal code took special care to protect children from seduction, for which the penalty was the death sentence or a heavy fine.

Roman literature shows homosexuality as a subject of amusement or contempt, and indeed, the satires of Juvenal and the writings of Petronius attribute to the ruling classes of the time every possible sexual vice. The Emperor Nero had Sporus, his favourite, castrated, after which he went through all the ceremonies of marriage and made the youth his wife.

Scientific literature on the less common forms of deviant behaviour is sparse. An early reference relates to one rare piece of deviant behaviour, namely pygmalionism, no doubt so named from the history of Pygmalion in the tenth book of Ovid's *Metamorphoses*. This is a poetic translation by Charles Hopkins written for the Duchess of Grafton and published along with the translation of Ovid's *The Art of Love* in 1782. The term *pygmalionism* comes from this particular story which relates to the love of a youth for an ivory statuesque nymph which presumably took the form of a fetishistic object and took on such realism for the youth that "fierce and boundless were his mad desires. He felt her flesh (his fancy thought it such) and feared to hurt her with too rude a touch. He kissed her with belief so strong and vain that he imagined how she kissed again."

In 1730 a book was published entitled *Plain Reasons for the Growth of Sodmy in England*. This book was published anonymously in London, and the author attributed the prevalence of this vice to the mollycoddling of boys and the cultivation of effeminate habits in young men. The author deplored the habit of sending young boys to schools run by women and felt that young men's habits of attire, continental manners, indolence and tea drinking and particularly Italian opera were especially pernicious since "it is well-known that sodomy is thought a trivial matter in Italy, so that no sooner does a stranger set foot in Rome than the procurers rush to ask if he wishes a woman or a young man!"

The earliest reference to exhibitionism discovered by the author (Haslam, 1976) was in connection with a communication from the Commission against Blasphemy dated 3 January, 1550, in which a man by the name of Domenego was accused of having repeatedly exposed himself to women in church during Mass. For this behaviour he was sentenced to six months in prison followed by ten years of exile from Venice and her territories (Bloch, 1914).

The fact that modern deviations appear only rarely in older literature does not imply their recent origin but rather that their appearance as criminal offences is relatively recent. The attention, therefore, of criminal and medical writers has only recently been turned towards them.

In England ancient common law did not consider such behaviour punishable, but many acts of this type were converted into offences by the Star Chamber and later by the Court of the King's Bench, which took over the function of *custos morum* after the restoration of the monarchy. This Court made acts of gross public indecency misdemeanours at common law in its judgment of 1663 in the case of Sir Charles Sedley, who was fined 2000 marks and imprisoned for one week for showing himself naked on a balcony and throwing down bottles among the people of Covent Garden (Rooth, 1970).

Book 4, Chapter 4 of Blackstone's commentaries, Section 11,

"offences against God and religion" states as follows: "the last offence which I shall mention more immediately against religion
and morality and cognisable by the temple courts is that of open
and notorious lewdness either by frequenting houses of ill-fame
which is an indictable offence or by some grossly scandalous public indecency for which the punishment is a fine and imprisonment."

Section II

PARTNERSHIP PROBLEMS

Chapter 3

INTRODUCTION

IN THIS SECTION we will deal with a group of problems where a stable partnership has been created, often indeed, an emotionally satisfying partnership, but where the sexual performance, for various reasons, is impaired. Thus, it must be emphasized that these problems are partnership problems and any concepts formulated with regard to treatment of these conditions must take cognizance of this fact. This group of conditions may be sub-divided basically into three types. The condition of vaginismus or psycho-genic dyspareunia is confined to females, although dyspareunia due to physical causes can of course occur occasionally in the male. Secondly, there exist disturbances of ejaculation that are confined to the male. Thirdly, there are conditions of disordered erection and climax, generally referred to as impotence in the male and frigidity in the female, although many of the factors concerned are common to both sexes and both conditions, the emphasis naturally differing in terms of the anatomical and physiological variations displayed in the two sexes. There is much overlap and interplay between these groups; often it will be found that one partner may show a degree of malfunction in one respect while the other partner similarly shows a malfunction in another. Nevertheless, it is convenient to treat the conditions separately as each have distinctive symptom patterns.

A series in York, however (Haslam, 1975), showed that 30 percent of partners who attended a clinic for psychosexual disorders themselves had a sexual dysfunction in addition to the one referred as the "patient."

In avoiding impotence and frigidity as terms, therefore, the conditions will be described firstly as erective and orgasmic dysfunctions. These may occur in male and female and may be primary or secondary, partial or total.

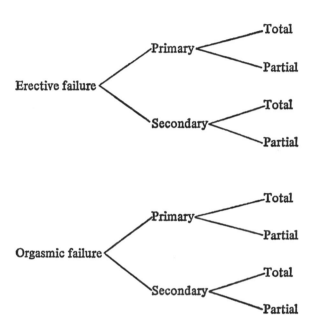

Secondly, ejaculatory dysfunctions will be considered. These may be of two types: premature ejaculation, which is common and often associated with partial erective failure; and orgasmic failure in the female and ejaculatory delay or failure, which is rarer.

Finally vaginismus will be considered, where muscle spasm of the pubococcygeus muscles is associated with a typical syndrome of response when any penetration is attempted.

Chapter 4

ERECTIVE AND ORGASMIC
DYSFUNCTION

IT IS CONVENIENT to discuss the main problems found in this
group of partnership disorders together since there is considerable overlap in both aetiology, symptomatology and treatment.
Also, although the male and female are anatomically different,
the similarity between the conditions is much more marked than
may be implied by use of the terms *impotence* and *frigidity*. In
practice, the disorders in both sexes can be considered as arousal
or orgasmic malfunctions.

In the male there is the added complication of the ejaculatory process, which is not found in the female, but this is virtually, in terms of the erotic process, simply the outward manifestation of male orgasm, since the two normally are completely coincidental. Thus, in both sexes it is possible for sexual arousal
to be delayed or inadequate. This will lead to absence or prolonged delay in reaching orgasm, since the response to the erotic
situation appears minimal. This will show itself in the female
as orgasmic delay and a complaint of frigidity. The lack of sexual arousal (which in the female will be demonstrated by enlargement of the clitoris and the transuding of lubricating fluid
from the vaginal glands) may go relatively unnoticed and be only
a secondary complaint.

In the male, however, with the external genitalia more prominent, lack of erective response is likely to be the presenting complaint, which is described as impotence. The orgasmic delay
resulting therefrom would be considered too obvious to mention.
Excessively rapid achievement of orgasm in the female is un-

likely to be a source of complaint since the female is physiologically capable of multiple orgasm and, in any case, orgasm in the female does not prevent further sexual activity between the pair. In the male, however, orgasm with ejaculation too early is likely to be a source of complaint since the erective detumescence in the male following ejaculation will be a source of dissatisfaction to the female if climax has not been reached.

Thus seen from this point of view, it will be noted that the sex differences in the male are basically simply those dictated by differences in performance capability. At this stage, however, the sexes diverge slightly, since the problem of premature ejaculation (because of the physiological mechanisms associated with this state) shows certain features which distinguish it from straight orgasmic change as found in the female.

It will be recalled that mechanisms associated with sexual arousal, ejaculation and orgasmic release are associated with the autonomic nervous system and, in particular, the sympathetic and para-sympathetic nerve supplies in the lumbo-sacral area. At risk of over-simplification, it can be briefly said that the para-sympathetic nerve system is concerned with the production and maintenance of erective response, whereas the sympathetic system is associated with the ejaculatory response. Since the para-sympathetic system is basically a "chewing-the-cud" system concerned with relaxation and the internal activities of body physiology and since the sympathetic system is concerned with the "fight-fright-flight" mechanism of muscular arousal and in particular, the mediation of anxiety responses, it will be seen that for the successful erective response in both sexes, the para-sympathetic system must be working effectively and a relaxed atmosphere should be the ideal. Similarly, the over-activity of a sympathetic nervous system in a state of anxiety or tension is likely to produce early ejaculatory response but, in addition, because the sympathetic and para-sympathetic nervous systems are mutually antagonistic, the one tending to suppress the other, it will be seen that in a state of anxiety, the para-sympathetic system and the ability to achieve satisfactory erection are likely to be diminished.

This is the key not only to the formation of a large number

of erective and orgasmic disorders but also to their perpetuation and worsening through a vicious circle. This is well described in Masters and Johnson's textbook, the principal point emphasized being that of performance anxiety and the creation of a state whereby the individual becomes an observer of his or her performance. Thus, the male is saying to himself: "I hope that my erection will be satisfactory tonight. I hope that I will not ejaculate too early." And his very fears on this point are likely to worsen the already strained performance situation. Similarly, in the female the fear "Will I become aroused, will I reach orgasm tonight? Will I manage to get there before my husband ejaculates or will I be left in the air?" equally increases her anxiety and effectively delays erective and orgasmic responses.

While this explains the self-perpetuating mechanism of secondary anxiety, the aetiology of the primary disability must also be considered, though often this proves to be a trivial episode, the basic causes of which have long since disappeared. These can be, for example, such simple factors as honeymoon nerves, difficulties with a contraceptive technique, a surfeit of alcohol, a situation which produces guilt feelings, fear of discovery, or a host of other straightforward problems. Many of the aetiological factors concerned in male and female sexual inadequacy have been reviewed by Cooper, who has written widely on the subject in a number of journals (1969c & d). There is a very large literature on the aetiology of male potency disorders which can be subdivided into organic, constitutional and psychogenic theories. These latter factors are considered to be the most dominant, and both psycho-analytical and behaviourist views have been put forward, the most frequently asserted psychogenic causes being anxiety, resentment, disgust, inversion, inhibition and ignorance. The most important further factor is the presence of functional psychosis, in particular an early and undiagnosed depressive illness.

In addition to anxiety-induced erective failure, two other fairly straightforward problems frequently occur.

In the older man erective failure may be produced after a period of prolonged abstinence. This not infrequently occurs when such an individual becomes widowed, and perhaps in the sixties marries again after a period of five years or more of being aclimactic. A younger man is not likely to be in this situation since he will in all probability obtain a new partner more quickly and, if not, will probably practise masturbation. In any event, he is younger and fitter in his general health.

The older man, however, will be less likely to seek self-relief. Just as a man may go on playing tennis or squash into his sixties if he has continued throughout his life, so the individual who stopped playing at forty-five and tries to start again at sixty-five will encounter serious problems. His muscles have lost their tone. His general physical fitness is reduced, and his body is less able to recover from this disuse atrophy.

To draw this parallel with sexual function seems not unreasonable. With disuse, the testosterone levels may fall and some atrophy of the testes can occur. Disuse atrophy of muscles will occur in any part of the body, including the tissues related to the genital tract. Certainly such men frequently find if they embark on a further relationship that erective failure may be a problem and the ability to ejaculate, which will have become less frequent with the passage of time, may be curtailed. If, in particular, they marry a younger wife and attempt to maintain an orgasmic rate appropriate to their younger days, then impotence may ensue simply from the mechanisms outlined above and from fatigue.

A not dissimilar problem may occur in the younger man who is attempting to be sexually more athletic than is his norm. To put it in simple terms, if a twice-a-weeker attempts to be a once-a-nighter, after a period of time on this higher level of output, he will tend to develop a period of relative disinterest and find the ability to maintain erection and ejaculate may be temporarily reduced. This in itself is no problem unless such an individual, failing to appreciate the reasons, develops anxieties about himself when the train of events of secondary performance anxiety outlined earlier and the vicious circle that can ensue starts to operate. Thus, the young man's failure to be aware of his body's capabilities and his wish to prove himself may lead to the development of the very thing he fears.

In the author's experience, more profound psycho-dynamics are a rarity. Repressed homosexual inclination is one obvious reason for poor performance with a female, and unresolved oedipal conflicts or inbuilt fears of the female or of the vagina may again induce psychologically determined impotence or ejaculatory failure. It is becoming appreciated, however, that a larger proportion of cases of erective failure is due to organic causes than had been realized heretofore.

The organic causes of erective failure can be considered under four general headings: (1) local conditions affecting the genitalia, (2) generalized disease, (3) hormonal disorders, and (4) problems produced by drug therapy itself.

Local Disease

Rarely genital abnormalities may play a part in the development of erective failure. Hypospadias, while it may produce problems of fertility or ejaculation, is rarely a cause of difficulty with erection itself.

In uncircumcised individuals excessive tightness of the foreskin may lead to pain on erection, and, if the foreskin is unable to be retracted, can occasionally lead to an emergency situation where circumcision is required to relieve the swelling and preputial inflammation that may develop.

Priapism is another emergency problem where, usually as a result of prolonged erection, where there is venous stasis sometimes worsened by the use of penile rings or aphrodisiac preparations containing yohimbine or strychnine, thrombosis occurs within the erectile tissue, and painful erection of the organ continues with detumescence unable to take place. Such a condition, if not relieved urgently, can lead eventually to unsatisfactory and painful erection due to resultant fibrosis.

Sometimes injuries to the shaft of the penis result in localized areas of fibrosis and give rise subsequently to a condition known as Peyronie's disease, which produces distortion of the shape of the penis on erection, again leading to pain and disturbed function. Such conditions can only be established by full

examination of the penis in both flaccid and erect states. Thus
in terms of psychosexual counselling, it is the after-effects of such
trauma that may be relevant, and in many cases of male dyspareunia a careful history should be taken of any such past events.

Infective processes, venereal or otherwise, can give rise to
symptoms of pain on intercourse. In particular, pain may be
felt at the tip of the penis from the results of a low-grade prosta-
titis.

General Disease

While any general disease which causes debility or chronic
ill health, such as severe anaemia, may cause some degree of
loss of libido, it is particularly that group which can produce a
peripheral neuropathy or can damage the autonomic nerve supply to the genitalia which is liable to directly affect sexual function.

In this work we are not concerned with small print diagnosis
but rather with reviewing the everyday problems which can present in psychosexual clinic work. A common difficulty is that of
diabetes. There is a well-recognized connection between diabetes and erective failure, particularly in those cases where the diabetes has been present some time and poorly controlled and a
diabetic neuropathy has developed. Such a neuropathy can
affect autonomic function as much as it can peripheral nerves.

However, it is equally true that there are many diabetics who
do not develop impotence, and there are many impotent people
who are not diabetic. The problem arises, therefore, in assessing the relative importance of diabetes along with other factors
when such a patient presents with a sexual problem.

If the sexual problem is due to the diabetes, then the only
practical treatment is to maintain as good control of the condition
as possible and avoid worsening. Often, the impotence is partial
and of slow onset, but it is quite common for secondary performance anxiety to develop on top of the original organic lesion.

An attempt should be made to diagnose positively. Thus,
other evidence of peripheral neuropathy should be sought, and
sensory changes in the genitalia, absence of the cremasteric reflex

and similar clues may be obtained.

Neuropathies may also be found in association with pernicious anaemia and subacute combined degeneration of the cord. Other common causes of neuropathy are associated with hypertensive disease and with chronic nicotine poisoning.

Disseminated sclerosis may affect sexual function through damage to the long tracts in the spinal cord and thus erective failure through para-sympathetic involvement or through a central defect. Syphilis in its later stages where tabes or G.P.I. supervene may induce similar dysfunctions. A generalized loss of libido may be found in thyroid deficiency and in pituitary disease.

Hormonal Disturbances

Relatively recent research has made it possible now to measure levels of testosterone, follicle-stimulating hormone (F.S.H.), luteinising hormone (L.H.) and prolactin in blood samples. Thus, it is possible to identify these abnormalities, particularly in males suffering from erective failure, who in the past would undoubtedly have been considered psychogenic. It is sobering to consider that throughout the history of medicine and particularly in psychiatry, dating from the days of demonology and before, the clarification of organic syndromes in many diseases has been preceded by a phase where the condition was ascribed to sin, malice or fecklessness.

While anxiety-induced disturbances of sexual function are extremely common, there are nevertheless some cases where a specific syndrome can be delineated, and no doubt in the years ahead, more of these will be discovered as biochemical techniques develop in sophistication.

Testoterone levels might be reduced in males as a result of maldevelopment of the testes, undescended testes that become non-functional or testes that are damaged as a result of infective or neoplastic disease, particularly in this context, the after-effects of mumps contracted in adult life. Damage can also occur from trauma or castration, and in older men there sometimes appears an apparently ideopathic decrease in testosterone levels. In cases where the testosterone level falls below the normal range, a loss of libido associated with erective incompetence can develop. In such cases treatment with testosterone replacement therapy can be highly effective.

In the female, distortions of F.S.H. and L.H. levels may again cause a disturbance in sexual function. While testosterone deficiency may be asymptomatic, it is usual to find in the female that there is a disturbance of menstruation leading to amenorrhoea. This gives a clue to the investigations required. Furthermore, oestrogen levels may be reduced post-menopausally and as a result of oöphorectomy, which in the past often seems to have been undertaken even in non-malignant cases and where replacement therapy has not been given, leading quite rapidly in some if not all cases to a loss of libido and orgasmic failure. This may be associated with changes in the vaginal wall where dryness results in dyspareunia. Oestrogen replacement here can rapidly effect an improvement.

Thirdly and more recently, there has been a developing awareness of the role which prolactin may play in both sexes quite separately from its role in milk production. Raised prolactin levels may be found in a variety of conditions. Prolactin levels appear to be directly related to dopamine metabolism; bromocryptine, which is a dopamine agonist, reduces prolactin levels directly. Many of the drugs used in psychiatry are dopamine antagonists and appear to produce their beneficial anti-psychotic effect through some action on this mono-amine system. This, in fact, produces a rise in prolactin levels and explains why some patients on phenothiazines develop temporary sexual dysfunction, since hyperprolactinaemia is associated with this failure of libido.

Phenothiazine drugs and tricyclic anti-depressants may therefore induce a hyperprolactinaemia through this dopaminergic mechanism. Anxiety itself can push the levels high, though not usually above 600 nmol/liter. The condition may be found ideopathically, but an important condition to eliminate is an adenoma of the pituitary gland. These are often benign microadenomata and induce a hyperprolactinaemia without showing any gross abnormalities on X-ray of the pituitary fossa. If they enlarge or are invasive, however, distortions of the pituitary fossa may be found on X-ray of the skull and can enlarge rapidly during pregnancy with resultant pressure effects perhaps causing disturbances in the visual fields.

Male hyperprolactinaemia may be asymptomatic apart from the disturbed sexual function, but occasionally a milky secretion exudes from the nipples. In the female, there is usually a distortion of the menstrual cycle and amenorrhoea, and often galactorrhoea in addition, though by no means always. Indeed the incidence of gallactorrhoea has been estimated at as little as 20 percent of those cases showing ideopathic hyperprolactinaemia. Treatment with phenothiazine drugs can, of course, induce such a galactorrhoea in some cases. No doubt this is the mechanism.

It is important, therefore, to investigate prolactin levels, particularly in cases of middle-aged onset impotence and in females with orgasmic failure associated with menstrual disturbance. If a high prolactin level is found, then serial estimations may need to be done to remove the anxiety effect, and X-rays of the pituitary fossa should be taken, serially for some months, if necessary. The symptomatic treatment of hyperprolactinaemia is the administration of bromocryptine, which will reduce the prolactin levels back to normal and, in those cases where it is relevant, will improve sexual functioning within a short time.

Drugs

Iatrogenic sexual dysfunctions induced by drugs or medicaments taken for other conditions are becoming an increasingly important factor in the aetiology of sexual dysfunctions. Drugs which have an action on para-sympathetic or sympathetic nerve conduction and their synaptic mediators, noradrenalin and acetyl choline may interfere with ejaculatory response in the male through the lumbo-sacral sympathetic outflow and equivalent orgasmic disturbances in the female. Over-activity of this system may cause premature ejaculation coupled with partial impotence since the sympathetic and para-sympathetic systems are mutually antagonistic. Drugs affecting acetylcholine and the para-sympathetic system are liable to cause disturbances of arousal and interfere with the normal functioning of erectile tissue, therefore producing partial erectile failure in the male and orgas-mic and erective failure in the female.

Drugs may also act centrally. Mono-amines, in particular dopamine and serotonin, are involved through their activity in centres in the limbic lobe, which can in turn cause a diminution of autonomic response. Dopamine antagonists have already been mentioned as reducing sexual drive. The role of oestrogen and thus the effect of the contraceptive pill may also be important in the aetiology of some cases of loss of libido. The mechanism appears to relate to sensitivity to mono-amines in those with raised oestrogen levels; it is worth noting that there appears to be some interaction between tricyclic anti-depressants and the contraceptive pill, whereby the effect of the latter may be dimin-ished.

A further group of drugs which may affect sexual function is the hypotensives, and in particular those where there is a cen-tral effect on dopamine metabolism in such drugs as methyldopa, and possibly also at a peripheral level in those drugs which are beta-blocking agents such as propranolol.

Some of these problems can be complex. For example, the patient suffering from a mild depressive illness, one of the symp-toms of which may be reduction of libido, may then be treated with an anti-depressant which, while causing relief of the depres-sive syndrome, has the additional effect of decreasing arousal through its side-effects. The addition of performance anxieties resulting from these disturbances may lead to a very involved picture. Similarly, patients presenting with hypertension may have a disturbance of sexual arousal associated with a neuropa-thy. The addition of hypotensive medication may induce depres-sive features since some hypotensives are well recognized as caus-ing this, reserpine in particular. This depression may in turn reduce further the sexual drive, and the hypotensive drug may produce an ejaculatory dysfunction. Performance anxieties may again appear, leading to a picture which takes considerable re-solving.

The tricyclic anti-depressants act by making mono-amines more available from the stores at the synapse. Their atropine-like side-effects are of nuisance value and can include ejaculatory delay and orgasmic failure in the female. Indeed, imipramine has been used in the treatment of premature ejaculation by attempting to induce just this delay. Levels of arousal may not be affected, but climax previously induced without difficulty may now be impossible.

Some of the newer anti-depressants such as the oxazines and tetracyclic compounds are likely to be less of a problem in this respect.

Mono-amine oxidase inhibitors are also used in the treatment of depression and some phobic states act by the inhibition of mono-amine oxidase and by inducing a longer effectiveness of mono-amines at the synapse. These drugs can cause disturbances of ejaculatory function, sometimes producing ejaculation without erection or a failure in the normal expulsion of the ejaculate. There may be complete ejaculatory failure or reflux ejaculation into the bladder. In the female there is again orgasmic failure in some cases.

Butyrophenones, of which benperidol is an example, are used as major tranquillizers but also have been used for their anti-erotic effect in reducing sexual drive in those with deviant sexual behaviour. Finally, anti-androgens such as cyproterone, which may also be used for this purpose, induce a long-lasting diminution of sexual drive associated with sterility.

The question of the relevance of androgenic steroids and oestrogens and their possible deficiency in the causation of sexual inadequacy must be briefly reviewed. There is no doubt that deficiency of oestrogen following oöphorectomy may cause diminution of libido in the female, and the same has been found in the male after castration (witness the employment of eunuchs in classical and mediaeval times). This finding, however, is not universal, and it is in any case a rare complication of any psychosexual problem. Androgens have alleviated constitutional and secondary eunuchoidism (Koch, 1936). Oestrogen has been shown to reduce male libido, but the reverse is not the case with androgen in the female. Ismail (Cooper, 1969c) has shown that a group of impotent men had a very significantly reduced urinary testosterone level compared with a sexually adequate active group of comparable age. This level may, however, reflect sex drive rather than having any prime significance in causation (Ismail and Harkness, 1967).

Werner (1939) found that male patients with symptoms comparable to the female climacteric showed a great decrease in potency. Many of them responded to testosterone.

With regard to factors of constitution and personality, Johnson (1965) and Tanner (1955) have expressed the view that the effects of early experience may make a marked contribution to subsequent sexual ability. Socrates in 400 B.C. was one of the first to suggest that constitutional elements might be important in determining sexual vigour (Jones, 1948). Congenital varieties of impotence were included in the ancient Hindu classification of sexual disorders, and more recent work by Kinsey has suggested that the response of an impotent patient to treatment was limited by his sex drive, which being innately determined, could not be significantly altered. Johnson also demonstrated that aspects of physique which purport to reflect relative degrees of maleness and femaleness, for example the androgeny score, showed a significant tendency towards gynandromorphy or femaleness in impotent patients, particularly in early onset impotence.

Cooper (1969d) has studied personality factors in female orgasmic disorders and concluded in a study of forty-one female patients with a primary disorder of frigidity that high anxiety scores and grossly elevated and intropunitive hostility scores in the neuroticism scale questionnaire and I.P.A.T. were found, and the hostility scale of Faulds, Cheyne and Creasey was markedly raised. There was no other significant distinction, however, between this group and the scores of normal individuals.

Much superstition has surrounded the possible causation of male sexual inadequacy, and many early references are quoted in Cooper's article. Mediaeval demonological literature presents the views appertaining to that era. In particular, the *Malleus Maleficarum* first published in 1849 gives much detail on the subject (Sprenger and Kremer, 1928). Sexual excesses of all kinds have been associated with impotence. This is found in Hindu medical text (Wise, 1945) and in Chinese literature of the golden period 1000 B.C. to 1000 A.D. (Wong and Wu, 1936). Indeed, Rush (1830) states "When indulged in undue or promiscuous intercourse with the female sex or onanism may produce seminal weakness, impotence and death."

Earlier a publication by Tissot along with a paper published anonymously in the eighteenth century in England entitled *Onania or the Heinous Sin of Self-Pollution* had condemned masturbation as a source of many bodily and mental ill-effects, particularly impotence. This was applauded by the religious views at the time and was taken up by and influenced medical thinking for many years, giving rise to the perpetuation of the masturbation insanity myth only dispelled in the last forty years. Indeed, more recent literature has tended to point more to a frustration syndrome with many of the symptoms previously ascribed to sexual excesses being more commonly found in those who live in enforced sexual frustration through lack of suitable guilt-free release for their drives.

More recent work, however, by Cooper, Masters and Johnson and others has shown that feelings of inadequacy and anxiety concerning performance (and particularly the secondary anxiety mentioned above), latent homosexual feelings, early conditioning from strict religious taboos and constitutional and personality factors, particularly related to other excesses such as overindulgence in alcohol or drugs, are much more important in the aetiology of these psychosexual disorders.

Of particular importance in relationship to disorders more prevalent in western society, both of sexual inadequacy and of sexual deviancy, are works by anthropologists such as Margaret Mead which have shown that many disorders of function are a product of the social circumstances in which the individual grows up and matures and lives and that these considerations should be taken into account before drawing any conclusions as to the factors which are important in problems of this kind.

In summary, therefore, it is important that when the physician is confronted with a case of sexual inadequacy, he should take a full history and make a thorough examination in order that the rarer possibilities may be excluded. Thus, attention to organic disease as outlined above and a brief number of sideroom tests to eliminate these possibilities should be undertaken. It is essential that a history be obtained from both partners, and ideally the couple should be interviewed both separately and together in order that a full appraisal can be made. A questionnaire is often a useful way of obtaining information from patients who may initially be ill at ease; Masters and Johnson in their book on human sexual inadequacy outline a history-taking format for this purpose. In this way, particular cues to the possible aetiology in psychological terms can be derived and these aspects can then be concentrated upon in further discussion.

It is essential in the history to obtain a very clear idea of exactly what the condition is and exactly when and in what circumstances it first occurred. The partner's reactions to the problem should also be elicited, and in this way it is possible, for example in a case of erective incompetence, to establish whether the condition is primary or secondary and whether it is total or partial. Thus, the following questions need to be asked: (1) Does the patient at this time ever obtain a satisfactory erection (a) under conditions of intercourse with his partner? (b) under similar conditions with any other partner? (c) under any abnormal conditions such as with a partner of the same sex or in response to erotic or pornographic literature? (2) Do erections ever occur in response to dreaming? (3) Are morning erections ever present, i.e. on waking? If all the answers to these questions are in the negative, it is important to establish the last time normal erection did occur, if ever, and under what circumstances it has occurred in the past. The same type of questions can be designed to elicit the circumstances surrounding ejaculatory dysfunction and orgasmic dysfunction in the female.

Having elicited a careful history, it is vitally important in the diagnostic appraisal that a physical examination should be carried out. This is perhaps to state the obvious, but many cases have been seen at the clinic in York where marital and sexual counselling have been carried out by other agencies and where, because the therapists were not medically qualified, a proper diagnostic physical examination had not been attempted. In a number of such cases glaring anomalies have been missed. Furthermore, physical examination is an opportunity for the therapist to reassure patients as to the normality of their genitalia. There is frequently an unvoiced fear on the part of many individuals that their organs are too small, ugly or misshapen in some way. For satisfactory sexual functioning, the patients need to have acceptance that they are both wholesome and touchable. Taboos are still surprisingly frequently encountered, and ignorance about their own anatomy and inhibitions about exploring the same are not infrequently found.

The physical examination, therefore, should perform two functions. Firstly, the presence of relevant general physical or psychiatric disease should be established if present. To this end a brief examination of the central nervous system, particularly looking for neuropathies if these are suspected, should be carried out. The blood pressure should be assessed to eliminate hypertension.

Secondly, a local examination of the genitalia is made. In the male this will include an examination of the testicles to note their presence and size, a note as to the presence of normal secondary sexual characteristics such as hair growth, and examination of the penis itself. Here one should observe the normality of the urethral meatus, the presence or absence of foreskin and the shape of the shaft. In uncircumcised individuals the foreskin should be retracted and a note made of the presence of any infection. If the question of history of priapism or Peyronie's disease is raised, then the penis should also be examined in the erect state. This may also be necessary and sensible in the investigation of some cases of impotence, but before it is attempted the circumstances should be carefully explained to the patient and a consent form signed. Examination of the ejaculate may also be helpful.

In cases of impotence, an assessment of night erective function as measured by a nocturnal penile plethismograph may be indicated. The plethismograph is a device designed to measure penile tumescence. The study of nocturnal penile tumescence (N.P.T.) and its association with R.E.M. sleep dates back to Ohlmeyer (Ohlmeyer et al., 1944) and his experiments of some thirty years ago. Ohlmeyer noted a cycle of nocturnal erection occurring on the average every 79 minutes during sleep. Periods of erection lasted an average of 25 minutes, and during an average sleep period, therefore, some four erective phases occurred. It is also noted that erection cycles occur during daytime sleep with similar characteristics, and Halverson (1940) independently described erections in sleeping infants and noted that they most often occurred during periods of heightened restlessness.

The relevance of such studies to sexual dysfunctions is that in wholly organically determined conditions, nocturnal penile erective response is not found. The corollary of this is that if nocturnal penile tumescence is exhibited, then the organic pathways must be intact.

This work has been reviewed by Karacan et al. (1975) in papers on nocturnal penile tumescence.

The original workers employed a contact ring which was fitted around the penis. This ring triggered a response on a kymographic recording when penile erection reached a certain minimum degree. It did not allow the determination of changes in degree of tumescence during the course of erection.

In the early 1960s, Schapiro adapted a commercially available mercury strain gauge for the measurement of penile erection. The gauge was placed behind the glans of the penis recording penile tumescence. Changes in the circumference of the penis produced a lengthening of the mercury-filled tube and consequent small changes in electrical resistance. These changes in resistance were amplified to produce calibrated linear changes on an E.E.G. tracing.

As an alternative, a small thermistor could be applied to the surface of the penis, and changes in penile skin temperature accompanying erection could be reflected by changes in the resistance of the thermistor. The thermistor was small enough so that the risk of local stimulation of erection was considerably reduced.

These and other methods are described by the authors mentioned above. Their research into normal sexual response shows that the vast majority of normal healthy males between the ages of three and seventy-nine exhibit such an erectile sleep pattern. They postulate that the ubiquity of nocturnal tumescence in humans seems to suggest that it has some vital functional significance for the organism. Similar evidence in females shown by Cohen and Schapiro (1970) and by Karacan himself has been provided, and similar activity has been shown in some other primates.

The data presented by these workers shows that variations in age have a significant effect on the expression of nocturnal penile tumescence. The total amount of time spent in tumescence increases from the age of three to a maximum of approximately 200 minutes during the pre-pubertal years and from that point gradually declines to a minimum level of approximately 100 minutes during an average night's sleep in the seventy-year-old age-group. When total tumescence time is expressed as a percentage of sleep-period time, the trend is similar. It is suggested that the high corollation between tumescence and REM sleep provides support for psycho-analytic conceptualisation of dreaming as a state for the release of instinctual drives, though others have preferred to view tumescence as an additional manifestation of autonomic activity.

Thus nocturnal penile tumescence represents an index of sexual function. The fact that intercourse has taken place relatively shortly before the sleep period does not appear to effect any changes in tumescence which could be attributed to this prior activity. Following a period of abstinence, there appeared to be fewer erections and a longer period of time between erections, though these changes were relatively slight. However, those tested by Karacan were young married people. Anxiety or aggression in the dream content seemed to be accompanied by sharp detumescence or sustained partial tumescence, and eroticism in the content was associated with an increase in tumescence.

Since anxiety is commonly a prominent aspect of the symptomatology of impotence, one might anticipate that nocturnal tumescence in impotent males would reflect this fact. Jovanovic (1972) examined a large number of impotent patients of various aetiologies and found a reduction in the length of tumescence episodes and in their frequency. It has been shown by Karacan in a study of diabetics that those patients who exhibited at least some degree of nocturnal tumescence had a good prognosis for return of potency when the diabetic symptoms were controlled. But patients who exhibited virtually no nocturnal tumescence were less likely to regain potency following control of other symptoms.

The construction of an inexpensive transducer for quantitative measurement of penile erection has been described by Karacan in an article in 1969 and another by Bancroft et al. in 1966.

An N.P.T. monitor is at present available for some $1,400 from Minneapolis, Minnesota. Such an instrument is useful in the assessment of suitability for internal prosthetics in cases of organic impotence.

Similar research instruments are available for measuring vaginal activity in the female; these have been developed in Britain, particularly by Pat Gillan working at the Maudsley Hospital (1977). This instrument, however, is still largely a research item (Cohen and Schapiro, 1970; Karacan, Rosenbloom and Williams, 1970).

Pursuing the factors important in diagnosis, the investigation of the case should proceed following physical examination and the use of plethismographs as described above to sideroom tests.

It is desirable to obtain a urine specimen and investigate for the presence of sugar and protein. It is important for reasons described above to eliminate the presence of diabetes and severe renal disease; such a screening procedure achieves this.

A blood-screening procedure which is found useful in York is to investigate the full blood count and erythrocyte sedimentation rate (E.S.R.). This eliminates the possibility of severe anaemia and pernicious anaemia; the presence of a normal E.S.R. removes the possibility of many collagenoses and chronic inflammatory conditions which might be relevant and require further general investigation. Thus the E.S.R. does not prove diagnosis but its normality removes the necessity for further more elaborate investigations.

An investigation of hormonal levels is appropriate in some cases. In particular, testosterone levels should be estimated in all patients presenting with impotence in middle age or where there is any evidence to suggest the possibility of reduced testosterone output. In the female, oestrogen levels may require to be estimated for similar reasons, particularly in the patient who has had oöphorectomy or is post-menopausal and where symptoms suggestive of oestrogen deficiency are complained of. F.S.H. and L.H. levels should be estimated in those in whom there is an abnormal pattern of menstruation.

In both sexes the estimation of prolactin is now desirable. In the male this should be carried out in those presenting with middle-aged onset impotence or where there are any signs suggesting abnormalities of pituitary function, alterations in intra-cranial pressure or the presence of any breast secretion. However, hyperprolactinaemia is frequently asymptomatic, and since treatment is simple in uncomplicated cases where the prolactin level can be returned to normal through the administration of bromocryptine, this relatively infrequent but not insignificant cause of sexual inadequacy should not be overlooked.

In the female, it is probably only necessary to do such an investigation if there is an abnormality in menstruation, the presence of breast secretion or other suggestive symptoms. If the periods are completely normal, it is unlikely that prolactin levels can be seriously altered.

In making such an estimation, the role which anxiety can play in the temporay elevation of prolactin levels should not be ignored, since otherwise false positives may be found and unnecessarily acted upon. If the levels are not all that high (for instance in the region of 700 or 800 nmol/liter), then serial estimations should be made with the patient in a non-anxious frame of mind. If levels approach 1000 nmols or more, however, it is prudent to investigate the causes through further tests and a lateral skull X-ray and possibly even tomograms to assess the pituitary fossa.

Consideration will now be given to each of the sub-groups within the general classification of erective and orgasmic dysfunction.

Primary Erective Incompetence

This condition is defined in an individual who has never been able to achieve and/or maintain an erection sufficient in quality to accomplish successful coital connection. By this definition, therefore, it is a condition applying strictly to the male who requires erective ability in order to insert. This is a distinction of considerable practical importance, since erective failure in the female, although dissatisfying to the individual, does not prevent intercourse taking place, and the female in this circumstance at least is not subjected to the humiliation of failure all too apparent in the male who loses erection at the critical moment when penetration is attempted and from which the main source of secondary anxiety arises.

Primary erective failure may be associated with a variety of aetiological factors. Distaste of the act or fear of its consequences, unresolved oedipal situations or the presence of homosexual identification, but more frequently just straight nervousness, may be implicated. The initial failure may occur as a result of socio-cultural situations. For example, the pressures of the wedding night and all its build-up, a surfeit of alcohol before retiring and finally, in the virgin male, some difficulty through inexperience in rupturing the hymen may lead to a perfectly simple failure of erection. To the outside observer this would be very understandable, but to the couple in this situation it may be the cause of great alarm to one or both partners. While this situation itself may not recur, subsequent anxiety makes the male an observer of his own performance, and his subsequent fears and self-critical analysis of his achievement may, with subsequent failures, provoke more and more anxiety which, in turn, perpetuates the problem. Thus, the condition is maintained through the results of secondary anxiety, and although the original problems settle down, there remains an alteration in the psycho-social attitudes and anxiety about performance which itself perpetuates delay in adequate arousal. Treatment must be aimed therefore at this anxiety since the original trigger may long since have lost its significance.

Secondary Erective Incompetence

This condition implies a previously satisfactory coital connection on at least one opportunity. Again, this may be partial or complete and may occur in certain partner situations and not in others. It is most important, however, that it be made clear that occasional episodes of erective failure are commonplace and of no particular concern. This experience will have occurred in a large number of individuals when fatigued or distracted or under particular circumstances, perhaps due to ill-health, and will be of no consequence to the individual as long as he maintains a balanced attitude towards the occurrence. Should unnecessary anxiety be provoked by an isolated incident of this kind, then, of course, it can lead to further problems simply through the operation of secondary anxiety as described before. When an individual male's rate of failure at successful coital connection approaches 25 percent of his opportunities, a clinical diagnosis of secondary erective failure must, however, be accepted. The distinction between ejaculatory problems and erective problems, i.e. impotence, is an important one since although the two may coexist, they may have no direct relationship. When the premature ejaculator loses his erection, he does so as part of the male's total orgasmic response. The impotent male, however, if he succeeds in obtaining an erection, may shortly lose it but does so without any orgasmic or ejaculatory release. There is thus a loss of reproductive efficiency which sometimes, unfortunately for the female partner, does not occur in the premature ejaculator.

The aetiology of secondary erective failure is varied, and it is in this condition, particularly when occurring in middle age, that the more common physical and functional psychiatric causes of erective failure need to be considered and eliminated. It is also, however, in the middle-aged patient where the increased demands placed on a system which is past its most active may cause a breakdown in ability. Thus, the female who, on reaching menopause, feels herself to be safe from further pregnancy may increase her demands for sexual satisfaction, and the aging male, while capable of lasting longer than his more virile junior counterpart will probably find that the ability to repeat erection and orgasm as frequently as he did in youth is on the wane.

An established pattern of premature ejaculation prior to the onset of symptoms of secondary erective failure was recorded in 63 of a total of 230 men evaluated by Masters and Johnson. Secondary impotence as a direct result of episodes of acute alcoholic intake were found in 35 men. Acute trigger situations of a psychological kind were the third most frequently found group. Homosexual associations were found in 21 individuals. Only 7 cases of physiological dysfunction were found in their series, though, in addition to this group, a further 20 cases suffered from diabetes.

Primary Orgasmic Dysfunction

This condition is defined as a state in which a woman has never, under any circumstances, developed an orgasmic response either in circumstances of sexual intercourse or through other methods of arousal such as masturbation or as part of a dream.

In our culture the woman's role in sexual matters has been rather more strictly determined than the male's role. Such socio-cultural influences often place a woman in a position in which, she must adapt or inhibit and distort her natural capacity to function sexually in order to fulfill her genetically assigned role. Thus, psycho-social and cultural factors are likely to be of much greater importance in determining the woman's ability to respond in certain situations. A second important factor not emphasized in the literature is that to achieve orgasmic response implies erective adequacy. Many of the cases where a complaint of orgasmic incompetence is made may, in fact, show an erective fail-

Chapter 5

EJACULATORY DYSFUNCTION

Premature Ejaculation

THE REPRODUCTIVE BIOLOGY Research Foundation in St. Louis has defined premature ejaculation as that condition where the male cannot control his ejaculatory process for a sufficient length of time during intravaginal containment to satisfy his partner in at least 50 percent of coital connections. An adequate definition is difficult as it must take into account the socio-cultural orientation of the couple; the definition may fail to take into account the concurrent condition of orgasmic delay in the partnership. Often, however, ejaculation is so rapid as to occur at or before entry and the condition is then self-apparent. The reader cannot do better than to study the relevant chapters in Masters and Johnson's book that deal with each of these problems in turn in order to get a fuller understanding of the psychological factors involved.

Commonly, the condition occurs as a primary one in those males who have, prior to adopting heterosexual intercourse with a long-term partner, ejaculated under circumstances where rapidity was of no detriment. In secondary cases, the practise of coitus interruptus as a method of contraception is surprisingly commonly found, although when considering what must be happening with the long-term use of this method of avoiding pregnancy, it is perhaps not surprising that such a problem together with erective failure can easily develop, since the opportunity for normal satisfaction of either partner places undue emphasis on the ability of the male to control and delay orgasm, and his failure to do so is likely to cause an increasing build-up of nervous tension between the partners, particularly if the female fails herself to reach a climax in the process.

The usual result in a partnership where the male ejaculates prematurely is for the wife to become progressively more disinterested and dissatisfied with the sex act, since it rarely leads to satisfaction on her part. Thus, two things will happen: Firstly, the wife may make vigorous efforts to reach orgasm herself before her partner, which in turn is likely to make the premature ejaculator even more premature. Secondly, in order to delay ejaculation, the male may adopt a "freeze technique," where once entry has been assured, no movement must take place, and no handling of the penis must occur before entry for fear that this will trigger the ejaculatory response. This indeed may delay ejaculation, but this very pattern of behaviour tends to fix the response rather than to train the individual in control.

The condition can easily progress to secondary erective incompetence, particularly when the male is made aware of his inadequacy by a dissatisfied partner. The treatment of this condition calls for certain specialized techniques which must be learned between husband and wife. A general consideration of the treatment of all these conditions will be undertaken at the end of this section.

Ejaculatory Incompetence

This condition has much in common with the orgasmic incompetence found in the female, but the particular point here is the inability on the male's part to ejaculate intra-vaginally, although it is usually possible for ejaculation to occur extra-vaginally without problems. The condition may be primary or secondary, or it may be partial or total, that is to say, it may occur on some occasions and not others with a particular partner, or it may occur with one particular partner but not in other circumstances with other partners. For example, ejaculation may be possible with the regular marital partner but impossible with others due perhaps to guilt feelings or fear of disease. Equally, the reverse may be true, namely, ejaculation may be possible with a casual partner but impossible with the regular mate. This must be brought out confidentially in the history if satisfactory treatment is to be obtained. In Masters and Johnson's series, seventeen males were seen with this condition, fourteen being married. Twelve had never been able to ejaculate intra-vaginally during coition with their wives. In four this appeared to relate to a specific episode of psycho-social trauma. In five the notable feature was an upbringing of strict religious orthodoxy and the production of a sexual psycho-neurosis therefrom. Three men admitted to a physical aversion for their partner, and two appeared to relate to a fear of pregnancy.

Occasionally, it is found that secondary ejaculatory incompetence of a partial type had developed insidiously through the efforts of the husband to delay long enough to satisfy a partner who in fact suffered from orgasmic delay. The degree of control which the male achieves backfires when he finds that ejaculation for himself at times becomes impossible.

Total ejaculatory failure, both intra– and extra-vaginal, is very rare. As a secondary phenomenon it can occur after prostatectomy, as a response to neurological disease or iatrogenically from such drug therapy as mono-amine oxidase inhibitors. In the primary form when no organic problem of congenital type is found, deep-seated psychological problems can exist that can be very resistive to therapy.

Chapter 6

TREATMENT OF ERECTIVE, ORGASMIC AND EJACULATORY PROBLEMS

THE MODERN CLASSIC publication on the treatment of sexual inadequacies is the one by Masters and Johnson mentioned previously. They take their place in a line of distinguished scientists in western culture who have from Victorian times studied human sexuality and attempted to place treatment on a more rational basis. Havelock Ellis was the first of the Victorians to present modern views on sexual attitudes (Ellis, 1928). Van de Velde, a Dutch gynaecologist, also made an important contribution in his book *Ideal Marriage* in 1926 (Van de Velde, 1965).

The first great figure in the United States to study sexology was Dickinson, a gynaecologist who did much research into normal human sexual functioning (Dickinson, 1931). Kinsey's work has already been mentioned; a zoologist by training, he founded the Institute for Sex Research at Bloomington, Indiana in 1938 and wrote two treatises which have become internationally known on sexual behaviour in the human male published in 1948, and sexual behaviour in the human female published in 1953.

Masters and Johnson's major contributions have been in the supplying of factual information, since few real facts were known before they began their eleven-year study in 1954, culminating in their publication of *Human Sexual Response*. In terms of therapy, however, their two-week therapy programme has become the model on which the majority of non-analytical treatment programmes has been based, and their results as published have been excellent. The key to this has lain in their intensive two-week programme combined with a dual sex therapy team, allowing for a therapeutic group of four to work through the problems by discussion and education while the couple is enabled in their fortnight honeymoon conditions to work through the schemata which are advised.

Before the clinician need get involved in the complexities of such schemata, however, certain basic matters must be considered. These are set out as follows:

(1) A careful history must be taken from both partners as outlined above. This ensures that a really accurate diagnostic appraisal is made, which is essential if further therapy is to be satisfactorily achieved.

(2) A careful examination must be made, including any investigations necessary to eliminate the rarer phsysical complications and causes of sexual inadequacy.

(3) In light of the above knowledge, an educational interview is given to the couple, separately or together as seems desirable, going carefully into the anatomy and physiology of sexual function and paying particular attention to those areas where ignorance seems to have caused symptoms to be perpetuated. Diagrams are useful (Figs. 1, 2, 3 and 4).

(4) Straightforward counselling is given on simple matters such as the use of lubrication to ensure a more pleasant tactile stimulation and the use of alternative positions and alternative methods of stimulation to create the necessary improvement.

The essential ingredient of these interviews is that the couple is to communicate with each other in a relaxed atmosphere, often for the first time, and to learn about each other's needs, likes and dislikes. The opportunity may be taken to give advice on contraception and other matters which the couple may care to bring up. Clarification of the role which anxiety can play in perpetuating symptoms and the vicious circle which secondary anxiety can set up can be brought out. It must be emphasized that the problem is always a partnership problem, no one individual being predominantly to blame or predominantly the cause of the difficulty. Frayed marital relationships with frayed emotional attitudes, in this way, may be mended, and the couple may learn to come to terms with their individual good and bad points.

If at this stage the general practitioner feels that further problems need to be elucidated or that a simple programme of advice and counselling has not achieved a success, referral should be made to a clinic for psychosexual disorders or, if one of these is not available in the locality, to a specialist known to have a particular interest and talent in this direction.

While special methods are available and special techniques have been devised to treat individual syndromes, it must be emphasized that many of the problems encountered in sexual inadequacies have a common basis, and the treatment programme in many ways will be similar. There is little doubt that since the publication of Masters and Johnson's work and the concepts they have introduced for the rapid treatment of these conditions, results based on these methods have been shown to be far superior to those practiced by other types of psychotherapy. It is often valuable not only to discuss principles of treatment with the partners, but to suggest reading matter which they can, in addition, digest while at home. The textbook by Masters and Johnson is

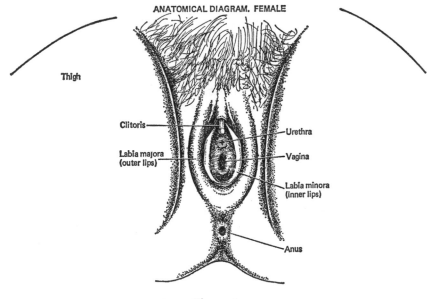

Figure 1.

not entirely suitable for this purpose being both too technical and too elaborate for the layperson's needs and couched in medical jargon. However, a translation of this work has been written by Belliveau and Richter (1970) in which the principles of treatment are outlined in a form suitable for the lay reader to comprehend. In this book a discussion on basic anatomy and physiology is introduced and the principles of Masters and Johnson's rapid treatment programme are outlined. Further chapters are then given on the individual problems encountered in particular syndromes. The principles involved in their treatment programme will be briefly outlined.

A basic premise of their therapeutic approach is that of the

ANATOMICAL DIAGRAM. FEMALE

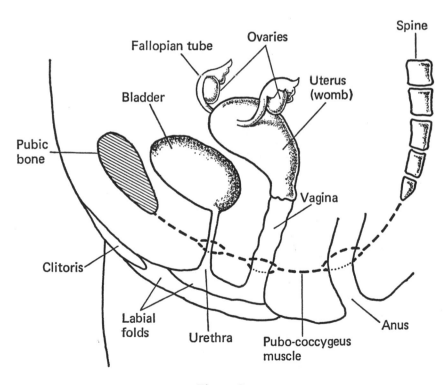

Figure 2.

conjoint marital unit. There is no such thing as an uninvolved partner in any marriage in which there is some form of sexual inadequacy. It is essential, therefore, that both male and female partners participate in the treatment programme.

It is Masters and Johnson's view that socio-cultural deprivation and ignorance of sexual physiology rather than psychiatric or medical illness constitute the aetiological background of most sexual dysfunctions, the implication being that a short-term educational effort combined with supportive psychotherapy is a reasonable approach to the treatment of sexual inadequacy.

Their results have been obtained by a paired sex therapy team, one of each sex working with each couple, which allows the husband and wife each to have "a friend in court" and an interpreter of the same sex who can support and explain a point of view without appearing biased. At the same time, the social rigmarole performed to impress the other sex therapist is mini-

ANATOMICAL DIAGRAM. MALE. RESTING

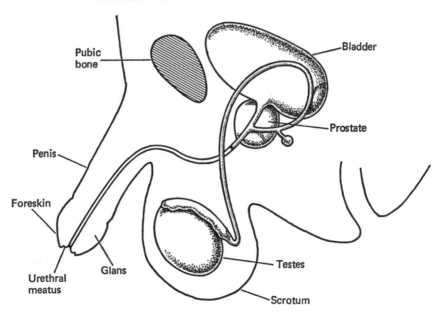

Figure 3.

mized.   In addition, transference feelings are better controlled.
Individual interviews of opposing sex pairs can be interspersed
or alternated as the need may appear.

    The key technique in this system as practised in the clinic
run by Masters and Johnson is for the partners to live in a local
hotel for two weeks.   They attend the clinic every morning and
work through a programme of discussion and gradual introduction to the concepts to be described below, while in the after-
noons they return to their hotel to practise the techniques which
they are to employ.   These ideal conditions may not often operate in circumstances appertaining to a health service in Britain,

ANATOMICAL DIAGRAM. MALE. ERECT PENIS

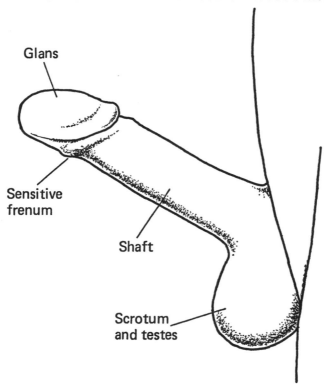

Figure 4.

but it would seem desirable to approach as near as possible this ideal by modifying it to suit the relevant circumstances of the individual therapists.

The therapist's role is to hold up a mirror to reflect so that the marital partners may see themselves as they are and to restate for the couple in an objective, unemotional way their problems, how they are hurting each other and how they are failing to communicate. It is essential at the start to abolish goal-orientated performance. One of the main tasks of the co-therapists is to remove from the patient at this stage the pressure to produce, perform or achieve. Fears of sexual performance in the marital bed are of major concern to both partners by the time voluntary treatment has been broached. With each opportunity for sexual connection, the immediate and over-powering concern is whether or not the individual will be able to achieve satisfactory performance. Thus the individuals become observers of their performance, and the secondary anxiety engendered (as has been previously explained) perpetuates the symptom.

The format for the fortnight is composed of round-table discussions and the introduction of the concept of "sensate focus," which was introduced in 1960 by Masters and Johnson at the beginning of their therapy programme. Basic to this concept is the recognition that touch is a vital part of personal human communication through which feeling can be conveyed. Regardless, therefore, of the couple's particular sexual problem, instructions are given to choose periods of time during the day when they will employ sensory exploration with each other. Directions are given to this end; the couple is told to return to bed at their hotel, where they should be naked, without distractions, and simply employ fondling, initially avoiding the specific erotic areas and using a moisturizing cream to improve the quality of the sensation. In due course, the pleasuring sessions include the erogenous zones, and as treatment progresses through the two weeks, particular problems are taken up in more detail, but continuing with a completely non-demanding atmosphere, until finally intercourse is attempted in phase III, using positions discussed (Figs. 5, 6 and 7).

Masters and Johnson's results are contained in a study of 510 married couples and 57 single people over an eleven-year period. There were 287 couples with only one dysfunctional partner, while the remaining 223 couples consisted of two dysfunctional partners. Of 790 individuals treated, 142 were treatment failures at the end of the two-week programme, an initial failure rate of 18 percent. Put another way, the initial success rate at the end of two weeks was 60 percent for primary impotence, 74 percent for secondary impotence, 98 percent for premature ejaculation

FEMALE SUPERIOR POSITION

Figure 5.

MALE SUPERIOR POSITION

Figure 6.

and for secondary orgasmic dysfunction 78 percent. At the end the success rate for primary orgasmic dysfunction was 84 percent and for secondary orgasmic dysfunction 78 percent. At the end of five years, a follow-up study showed an overall success rate continuing at 75 percent.

These results are excellent, and it is doubtful whether they can be bettered by any other therapeutic approach. It should be noted, however, that the fortnight's treatment is intensive and cannot always be applied in a health service. Furthermore, the selectivity involved meant that the patients taken on for treatment were highly motivated towards cure, certain patients being rejected initially because of lack of co-operation by one partner. In addition, the fact that patients were prepared to visit St. Louis and conform to the programme required implies in itself a high degree of motivation.

It is equally possible that some failures had an organic aetiology not possible to identify at that time such as hyperprolactinaemia.

REAR SIDE POSITION

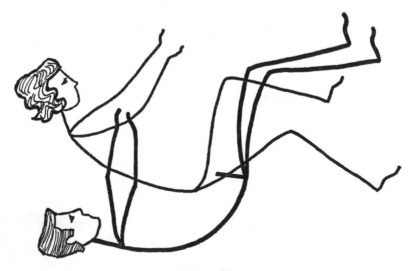

Figure 7.

In considering the individual syndromes, it is relevant to consider the work of other researchers in the field. Attempts have been made to elaborate on the clinical evaluation of treatment programmes, and other treatments besides that of behaviour-orientated psychotherapy have been attempted. Thus, when considering the question of erective incompetence in emphasizing the importance of an understanding of the neurological and vascular mechanisms involved, Tucker emphasizes the importance of excluding organic factors from disorders of the hypothalamus to local conditions of the genital tract. He recommends obtaining laboratory data to exclude syphilis, a protein-bound iodine test, cholesterol and liver function tests and, if necessary measurement of urinary 17-oxo-steroids and gonadotrophins.

Drug treatment for sexual inadequacies is usually of value only in relieving secondary anxiety. Thus, benzodiazepins may be used in small dosage, in particular lorazepam, and anti-depressants have been suggested to be of value, particularly in premature ejaculation. Drugs which purport to act as aphrodisiacs are by and large of value purely for their psychological effect, and replacement hormone therapy is of no value except in those cases proven to show a specific hormone deficit due, for example, to castration or local disease. Indeed, to give hormone treatment in those showing what is in fact a normal hormone output will merely result in suppression of the feedback mechanism, which will result in due course in the body producing even less of the natural hormone than it did before. Anti-depressants and other drugs for specific syndromes will, of course, be necessary in cases where the sexual disorder is secondary to some other disease process.

Belliveau and Richter emphasize that the treatment of impotence must devote itself particularly to the marital relationship, since an impotent man often views his wife as threatening to his self-confidence. She is the one person who knows the full extent of his failure and, if frustrated, may obtain some revenge by belittling her husband. These relationship problems must be ironed out in the round-table discussions. Later, sensate focus techniques must emphasize that there is no goal that the man must reach to be successful in this phase of treatment, and the partners will gradually give up their spectator role and focus instead on giving pleasure to each other. Once the man's erective pattern is established in a non-coital situation, genital stimulation is continued intermittently and, in due course, entry is attempted only after preliminary sex play, with the wife taking an active role and directing entry in the female superior coital position until this can be accomplished with ease and confidence (*see* Fig. 5).

Premature ejaculation has often been included in previous writings on the subject as an integral part of a discussion on impotence. The conditions are distinct and should be considered separately in terms of specific treatment procedures. Peberdy (1969) has emphasized the need for careful evaluation and recommends treatment with anti-anxiety medication with benzodiazepines, a mono-amine oxidase inhibitor which may be helpful in retarding ejaculation, and psychotherapy which should include advice on contraception, since this is commonly a factor in this particular problem. Imipramine and other tricyclic drugs have also been successfully used to assist in retarding ejaculation.

Treatment of premature ejaculation must devote itself initially to a re-education of the common fallacy that adopting a freeze and no-touch technique is a suitable way to attempt to delay climax. In fact, this perpetuates the problem and will, in any case, not be successful. Furthermore, this technique provides great difficulty for the female partner in terms of her own satisfaction, and her vigorous attempts to reach climax herself before the vital moment is past may also make matters worse. A man with premature ejaculation may try endless psychological and physical devices to break the pattern. Mental distractions or the use of anaesthetic creams and lotions may be employed. The distractions, of course, are unsatisfactory because they prevent enjoyment of intercourse in an uninhibited way. Furthermore, anaesthetic creams, while they may be partially effective in reducing sensation, may in turn lead to secondary impotence.

The essential feature, therefore, in the sensate focus techniques applied to this particular problem is to encourage the female to start fondling techniques of the male genitalia under non-demanding circumstances. Explanation must be given to the male that he must indicate to his partner to discontinue this activity before the point of ejaculatory inevitability occurs; each man will be able to recognize this point and can learn to stop before it is reached. After allowing the level of arousal to diminish, the woman must recommence fondling and continue again until it is indicated that she should stop. In this way, gradually improved control is achieved through familiarity with the experience. A particular technique which Masters and Johnson call "the squeeze technique" is employed as soon as the husband achieves full erection under these circumstances. This is described in the textbooks and can easily be learned by the female partner (Fig. 8). This procedure is effective in causing the man to lose the immediate urge to ejaculate and is employed on each occasion before ejaculatory inevitability occurs. After fifteen to thirty seconds, the wife continues manipulation again to full erection, and this procedure is continued for fifteen to twenty minutes during the practise sessions. At a later stage, coitus will be attempted with the woman maintaining control in this manner and controlling insertion through the female superior coital position once again, lifting herself and applying the squeeze technique until gradually improved control is obtained. Masters and Johnson have found that their results using this technique are excellent within a matter of a few days. Of seventeen men treated for ejaculatory incompetence in their series, only three were treatment failures.

Cooper (1969b) discusses the factors related to prognosis in disorders of sexual potency in the male. Schapiro (1943) recognized two discrete and aetiologically unrelated types of premature ejaculation: type A associated with erectile insufficiency and sexual hypotonus, and type B associated with abnormally high sexual tension. Treatment and outcome were different for the two conditions. Johnson (1965) found that recovery from a potency disorder was unlikely after three or four years. Masters and Johnson have not found that length of duration of a symptom was an adverse factor in prognosis.

Cooper, however, concluded from a survey of sixty-seven male subjects that 39 percent of the series had recovered or improved but 61 percent were unchanged or worse. Factors associated with poor outcome in this series were premature ejaculation, insidious onset, long duration, presence of personality disorder, absence of motivation for therapy, homosexual drive, lack of co-operation from the partner and increasing age of the male patient. It appears that insidious onset impotence in middle age often apparently not due to critical psychological factors but rather to an increasing disinterest in the subject and in the partner is a factor of importance in poor prognosis. It is in such cases that

SQUEEZE TECHNIQUE

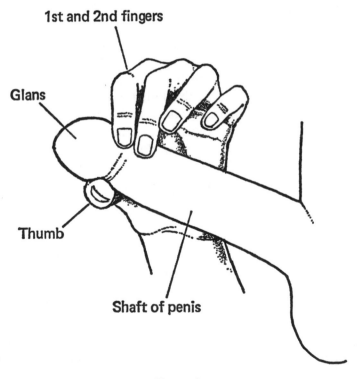

Figure 8.

hormonal disturbances should now be sought.

Turning to the treatment of sexual inadequacy in the female, Faulk (1971) briefly reviews the literature on the treatment of sexual frigidity and shows that some success has been obtained by a variety of methods including psycho-analytic interview (Abraham, 1956), insight therapy with physical self-examination (Dorkins and Taylor, 1961; Ellison, 1968), group therapy (Stone and Levine, 1950) and desensitization (Lazarus, 1963). Directive advice and counselling have been employed by Hastings (1967) and Masters and Johnson. In Faulk's series, just under half of the patients were substantially benefited, though this was a mixed group as orgasmic incompetence and vaginismus were both considered. Insight therapy was the method employed. Prognostic factors were discussed.

Cooper (1970) gives a review of forty articles on treatment and short-term prognosis of frigidity. In his series, fifty out of fifty-eight female patients attending the clinic with a primary disorder of frigidity satisfied a "treatment criterion" of attending for a minimum of twenty therapeutic sessions during one year. Treatment was by counselling and was effective in 52 percent of cases. It included training in muscular and concomitant mental relaxation, provision of optimum sexual stimulation for the female, sexual education and supportive psychotherapy. Cooper states that providing male potency is sufficient to ensure full penetration and delay orgasm for two minutes or more, the psychological status of the female and the smooth uninterrupted nature of the coitus are more important in improving female response. The prevalent male practice of interrupting coital thrust with the aim of delaying ejaculation in order that both partners may reach a climax simultaneously is more likely to inhibit female orgasm. He considers it a fallacy that females are innately slower than males in their sexual response, providing that stimulation is uniform and optimum for each.

Factors associated with a better treatment response included a duration of frigidity under two years, late onset dysfunction, heterosexual orientation, experience of pre-marital coitus to orgasm, feeling of affection towards male partner, normal personality and self-referral for treatment.

The psychotherapeutic component for treatment for the dysfunctional female must be to identify the requirements of the woman's existing sexual value system and to determine how these requirements are not fulfilled with her partner. Masters and Johnson state "the crucial factors most often missing in the sexual value system of the non-orgasmic woman are the pleasure in, the honouring of and the privilege to express need for sexual experience. In essence the restoration of sexual feeling to its appropriate psycho-social context is the reversal of sexual dissembling." The same sensate focus procedure is employed, but this time the emphasis is upon the male partner giving non-demanding stimulation to the female. By following through the treatment programme outlined in their book, Masters and Johnson had a success rate of nearly 80 percent in their series of 342 women.

Sexual Aids

The question is often asked as to whether those sexual aids often advertised and marketed by companies specializing in these devices are of value in the treatment of sexual inadequacy. A brief resumé of those commonly employed is included here, for completeness, but in the author's view, these devices are of more use in titillating the waning palate of a bored relationship or in adding variety to a stable relationship purely on a fun basis than they are of value in treating the type of disorder discussed above. Some devices are undoubtedly erotic in nature and may well be of value to some who require self-stimulation through lack of opportunity for emotional expression with a partner. However, their use in sexual dysfunction should only be recommended in very specific situations after careful exploration of the problem by a qualified practitioner with clinical experience in these matters.

Aids can be classified into particular types depending on the problem which they attempt to remedy.

Aids for Erective Incompetence in the Male

These consist of ring-like structures which can be placed around the shaft of the penis, constricting venous return and allowing the better maintenance of erection. They are often combined with soft protuberances which are said to cause increased clitoral stimulation and can, therefore, be used to improve stimulation to the female who experiences orgasmic delay. Phallic prostheses are also available which create the impression of erection by being used like a sheath over an otherwise flaccid penis.

These obviously have a limited use in those with physical deformities but do not correct the underlying problem in psychological terms. In addition, certain training devices are available which consist of sheaths which can be combined with a pump, thus promoting and maintaining erection by a suction effect. A further device marketed is known as the Blakoe® energizer ring. This is a device worn around the base of the penis, metal plates causing a small electrical stimulatory charge, which is said to tone up the tissues and no doubt also works by increasing the awareness of sensation in the genital organs of the male.

In those patients whose irreversible organic condition has led to total erective failure, it is now possible to use internal prosthetics that can be inserted under surgical intervention within the shaft of the penis itself, rather like a baculum bone present in the penis of some mammals. These gadgets vary in sophistication and price. The most simple ones are inserted as a rod-like structure from the base of the shaft. The snag here is that a permanent erectile state is produced, and while this may be more satisfactory to the female and certainly allows intercourse to take place, it has some difficulties for the male. However, the device is simple and for this reason less likely to go wrong; if rejection should occur, then it can be relatively easily dealt with.

Such devices have become considerably more sophisticated in recent years. Devices have been created which can be controlled so that erection can be produced or removed at will by using an inflatable penile prosthesis. Particularly for younger patients, the prospect of a perpetually erect penis may be as disheartening

as a permanently flaccid one. A number of these more complicated devices are now available; the one to be described here produced by American Medical Systems is not the only one on the
market. The difficulty with such complicated devices is that apart
from rejection, such mechanisms may from time to time go wrong
and require elaborate operative intervention to correct them.

The ideal prosthetic does not interfere with the patient's ability to experience orgasm and should be made of flexible materials
to be as undetectable as possible.

The A.M.S. device was developed in collaboration with researchers at the University of Minnesota Medical School and at
Baylor College of Medicine at Houston, the original research beginning in 1972. All the components of the I.P.P. (inflatable
penile prothesis) are totally implanted into the body so that only
the physician and patient need to be aware of their presence. It
is made of silicone elastomer and consists of cylinders, a fluid
storage reservoir and a pump. The two cylinders are implanted
inside the tunica albuginea adjacent to the spongy tissue of the
corpora cavernosa. A decision on cylinder length must be made
for each individual patient. These cylinders expand and contract as fluid is pumped into them and back into the reservoir.
The fluid storage reservoir contains a radio-opaque solution and is
connected to the pump by silicone tubes implanted in the pre-
vesical space under the muscles of the abdomen, a protected position where the patient is unaware of its presence. The pump
bulb is implanted to hang loosely inside the scrotal sac, its principal function being to transfer fluid from the storage reservoir
to the penile cylinders, which can be done when the patient
compresses the bulb in the scrotum. Thus the system produces
what is rather like a third testicle that, when squeezed (being sure
to squeeze the right one!), produces erection. Firmness of erection is determined by the number of times the bulb is pumped;
full girth erection can be achieved by pumping the bulb some
twenty times. When erection is no longer desired, a release valve
in the lower portion of the bulb permits the patient to evacuate
the fluid from the cylinders to the reservoir and restore the penis
to the flaccid state.

Conditions successfully treated in this way include diabetes, pelvic trauma, the after-effects of Peyronie's disease and priapism, arterio-sclerosis, multiple sclerosis, transverse myelitis and post-surgical impotence, for instance from prostatectomy or ileostomy.

The operative procedure requires a midline incision, and surgical time for the first implant ranges from two to three hours. Care must be taken with the patient's selection, since implantation of the prosthesis may damage or destroy latent natural spontaneous erectile capability. Post-operative complications, both surgical and mechanical, can occur: Malpositioning of the prosthesis within the corpora can result in buckling of the glans. Mechanical complications can include malfunction of the hydraulic mechanism, cylinder or tubing kinks and leakage of fluid due to degradation of the material or bonding failure. Non-symmetrical expansion of cylinders may occur because of excessive dilation prior to surgical insertion or inherent material weakness, which can cause bending of the shaft. Contra-indications to this particular prosthetic are a previous history of adverse reaction to Hypaque®, since this is used as a filling medium in the prosthesis.

Devices Used to Relieve Female Orgasmic Delay

These are usually devices placed on or around the penis to cause added stimulation to the female genitals by friction during intercourse. There are in addition training devices inserted into the vagina of the female causing improved tone to the muscles, which can be used as a practise procedure along with the artificial phallus. These are often known as duo-balls or geisha balls.

Vibrators

These are the most popular and commonly used devices and are available in a variety of forms suitable for stimulating the male or female genital tracts. Most work from a battery with a small motor causing a vibratory impulse which can be felt through the device. This produces a highly erotically stimulating effect on the erectile tissues and can be used as an aid in erective incompetence in the male or in the female. Viewed as an alternative method, the vibrator seems to be of some value to those who do not find it aesthetically distasteful. However, the use of artificial aids is often inhibiting to the couple by merit of their very artificiality, but if this inhibition can be overcome and they are used with intelligence and a certain sense of humour, then no doubt the couple can benefit in certain cases from the arousal so produced.

Chapter 7

VAGINISMUS

V AGINISMUS IS A CLASSIC example of a psycho-somatic illness
(Masters and Johnson, 1970). The principal feature is a
spastic contraction of the perineal muscalature (pubo-coccygeus)
surrounding the vaginal barrel. Confirmation of the diagnosis
can only be made by direct pelvic examination, when the pattern
of response is characteristic. The woman reacts in an established
pattern and shows marked nervousness, often attempting to escape
the examiner's approach by withdrawing towards the head of the
bed. The back tends to be arched, the abductor muscles of the
thighs are contracted and, when vaginal examination itself is attempted, there is a strong muscular spasm felt just within the vaginal outlet. When intercourse is attempted, this combination
of events makes the act impossible. It is quite frequently found
as an added complication when the male partner has certain fears
concerning his ability to consummate the act and may show a
partial erective dysfunction or premature ejaculation himself,
which may become more apparent with the successful treatment
of the partner.

Masters and Johnson have done much to clarify previously
distorted opinions on the subject of sexual inadequacy. They
consider a number of factors as being important in the aetiology
of vaginismus. They note a significant relationship with the following factors, namely: (1) concurrent male sexual dysfunction;
(2) excessively severe control of social conduct inherent in certain orthodox religious groups; (3) specific episodes of prior sex
ual trauma; and (4) attempted heterosexual function by a woman
with prior homosexual identification.

71

In the author's experience, the pain associated with attempted insertion into the vagina or even into the rectum is a common finding in the history of the patient. This may have been an attempt on the part of an examiner when the child was suspected of appendicitis; the application of a soapstick enema in the treatment of severe constipation; exploratory techniques on the part of the patient or friends in adolescence; early unsuccessful attempts at intercourse; or even unwanted sexual assaults such as attempted rape. Sometimes, however, none of these problems are found, and an explanation may lie in more deeply rooted psychological fears. Whatever the initial problem, however, a chain of events is set in motion so that a final maladaptive pattern of response develops with the classical triad of contraction of the perineal muscles, contraction of the adductors of the thighs and arching of the back occurring at any attempt by the male to obtain entry. Often the relationship may have remained unconsummated for some years since onset. An important feature in vaginismus is that the partnership, initially at any rate, is an emotionally satisfying one in other ways. Often sexual relief is obtained through mutual masturbation, and there is no loss of arousal to sexual approaches until the actual attempt at penetration takes place. This distinguishes the condition from erective and orgasmic dysfunctions discussed earlier.

An important further possibility must be considered when diagnosing a case of vaginismus, and that is the alternative diagnosis of dyspareunia due to physical causes. Technically dyspareunia refers to painful intercourse and implies that intercourse, though painful, has taken place to some extent. In this case, there will usually be a history of satisfactory intercourse prior to the onset of the condition. Vaginismus may be demonstrated as a secondary complication to the experiencing of pain on intercourse over a period of time. It may be appropriate, therefore, to review briefly the causes of dyspareunia before discussing the treatment of vaginismus itself.

In the female, the pain in dyspareunia can often be identified as being of a particular type, for example, superficial or deep. A complaint of pain on intercourse may quite frequently be psychological and can, of course, be used as an excuse to avoid sexual exposure. Commonly, however, the physical complaint, certainly if the pain is of superficial character, is due to simple causes such as a hymenal tag, a mild degree of vaginal irritation due to infection (for example, thrush) or more commonly an attempt at intercourse when the vagina itself is too dry. This common cause of pain is due, as a general rule, to inadequate sexual arousal before penetration is attempted. But in some women, even when satisfactorily aroused, the vagina is relatively dry; this problem can be easily corrected by the use of an artificial lubricant such as E.45®, KY Jelly® or ordinary Vaseline®. It goes without saying, of course, that the male partner should ensure that the female is adequately sexually aroused before penetration is attempted. Sometimes attempts on the part of the female to maintain herself in a state of cleanliness by the use of deodorants may itself cause excessive dryness of the vagina and lead to these problems, since often the deodorants contain anti-perspirants, which have a drying quality. Pain at the vaginal outlet, therefore, should be diagnosable by observation and a careful history, and the clitoral area should also be examined, as the finer localization of pain may not be very well defined. Smegma beneath the clitoral foreskin can cause chronic irritation. Adhesions beneath the minor labial folds anchoring the foreskin to the clitoral glans can cause distress when the foreskin is moved or pulled from its overhang position.

Occasionally sensitivity reactions causing vaginitis can develop due to chemical contraceptives, douches, the rubber itself or other agents.

Pain felt deep within the vagina may be due to a variety of causes such as pelvic infection, endometriosis or other intra-abdominal causes. A commonly overlooked problem in women who have born children is a traumatic laceration of the ligaments supporting the uterus. The basic pathology of the syndrome of broad ligament laceration is within the soft tissues of the female pelvis. The uterus is found to be in severe retroversion as a rule, and manipulation of the cervix shows a particular characteristic of movement. The pain is usually felt in any type of cervical movement, but particularly on pushing the cervix in an upward motion. The only effective treatment for this problem is operative.

It should be noted that dyspareunia can also occur in the male, which may result from hypersensitivity of the glans penis following ejaculation, from irritation by a retained foreskin, from smegma underneath the foreskin or occasionally from phimosis or urethritis. Occasionally, referred pain from the posterior urethra is found, and even more rarely, Peyronie's disease induced by induration and fibrosis of the corpora cavernosa of the penis and evidenced as an upward bowing can cause pain on erection. Occasionally downward bowing or penile chordee may be seen after trauma or gonorrhoea. Trauma can occur if the fully erect penis has been struck sharply downwards during intercourse by an over-vigorous partner, thus causing haematoma and often fibrous adhesions with healing. Pain may also occur from inflammation of the testicles, prostate or seminal vesicals.

It is thus important in a complaint of vaginismus to investigate for the possibility of dyspareunia due to other causes. The majority of cases referred to the psychiatrist, however, do not show any complication of this kind. But it is surprising how often simple causes of dyspareunia such as lack of lubrication or residual hymenal tags can be a problem which may well have been missed if adequate examination has not been made.

A characteristic chain of events is often found when the psychiatrist is presented with a case of vaginismus. Initially the patient has approached the family doctor, examination may well have been attempted but failed or has been partially successful, and the patient has been reassured of her physical normality only to find that no improvement has occurred. Referral may then be made to a gynaecological department. Here again, examination is attempted and may fail; the advice often given at this point is for the patient to come in for examination and dilatation under anaesthetic. Not surprisingly, in view of the nature of the condition, this examination proves completely normal, since the muscles are unable to go into spasm when the patient is unconscious. Dilatation with Sim's dilators may be attempted on the unconscious patient, and it is found that they pass easily. The patient is then awakened and sent home, again with reassurance or possibly even with a set of dilators with which she is told to practise. Again, it is often found that no improvement occurs. It is at this stage that the matter sometimes rests for months or years, and the marriage may well disintegrate. Surprisingly, perhaps, in a series of cases seen by the author, a small proportion had even become pregnant as a result of partially successful penetration, but even after delivery and return of the vaginal pelvic organs to normality, the condition had recurred. At some point along the line, referral to a psychiatrist may be made rightly on the assumption that the condition is, in a sense, psychologically determined. Even here the patient's troubles may not end because the condition, although very simply treated, is not always recognized or correctly approached by those unversed in the problem.

On the basis of certain analytical theories concerning the problem of vaginismus, attempts have been made in the past at using pure psychotherapy to relieve the problem. This, in general, is unsuccessful. Explanation and reassurance, however, combined with simple attempts at relaxation have been successful in many cases (Freedman, 1962; Mallesson, 1942).

The simplest and most successful treatment has been simple relaxation and the concomitant use of a deconditioning procedure with Sim's vaginal dilators. The technique is described in an article by Haslam (1965) and in practiced hands produces a 100 percent rate of success in two to eight half-hourly sessions, presupposing firstly that the diagnosis is accurate and secondly that the co-operation of the patient can be obtained.

Some authors have invoked the husband's aid in actively participating in the therapeutic procedure (Cooper, 1969a), as described in Masters and Johnson's textbook. The arguments for and against are probably similar to those for and against the husband watching the delivery of his wife's baby. Some will be supporters and some against the idea. In terms of the successful outcome of treatment it seems irrelevant, and in the author's experience, involvement of the husband in the active treatment phase is more a hindrance than a help. Probably the wife's preference should be the guiding line in the matter. Additional counselling with the husband is often needed at some stage, however, since a problem of premature ejaculation or erective incompetence may only become manifest with improvement in the wife's condition.

The routine adopted by the author is as follows: (1) A session is scheduled for history taking and initial examination to establish the diagnosis, along with an explanatory discussion with the patient aided by diagrams of the anatomy and physiology of the problem (Figs. 9, 10 and 11).

(2) Initial examination is carried out in a left lateral position, which makes it much more difficult for the patient actively to resist vaginal examination, and this is followed straightaway by the insertion of the smallest of the Sim's dilators, which is not much bigger than a little finger. It is practically impossible to prevent this being passed in the left lateral position. The author has found that a lighthearted approach to this matter, using, as a chaperone, a nurse familiar with the proceedings, is the best approach in order to win the confidence of the patient. Relaxation is confined to very simple measures; deep relaxation has not been found to be necessary.

(3) The patient is taught how to contract and relax the perineal muscles when the position is changed to the dorsal one. It is at this point that some resistance is often found. Reassurance and perseverance is necessary to ensure that the smallest dilator is inserted in this position. Once this has been achieved, the patient is often much relieved and can be shown how to move the dilator herself, to take it out and re-insert it. Confidence must be achieved with the smallest dilator before any attempt is made to move on. Should difficulties be found at any further stage, it is much better to return to a smaller dilator until confidence has again been restored. This should be achieved in the first and second treatment sessions.

(4) The next size dilator is used, again adopting the same approach. It is essential to use a large quantity of lubricating cream or jelly such as E.45®, KY Jelly® or a similar product during this

VAGINISMUS. EXPLANATORY DIAGRAM

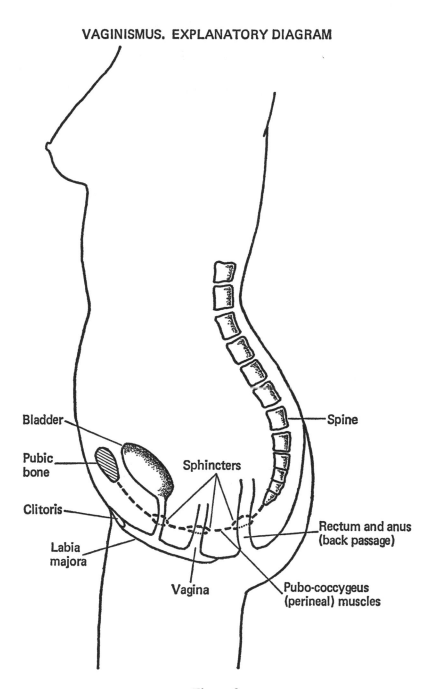

Figure 9.

process to ensure that the vaginal walls and orifice are well-lubricated to make passage of the dilators easy and pleasant. The dilators are gradually increased in size until, at the end, the largest dilator can be inserted with ease, both by the therapist and by the patient, in the dorsal position and in the kneeling position in the final session. This will take a variable number of sessions depending on the patient's confidence, progress and personality.

When this final step has been achieved and not before, intercourse may then be attempted. The patient is advised, on the first occasion, to consider her husband as a number 6 dilator that happens to have a man on the end. She should take the

VAGINISMUS. WRONG POSITION

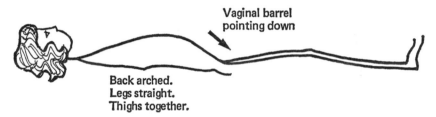

Vaginal barrel
pointing down

Back arched.
Legs straight.
Thighs together.

Figure 10.

VAGINISMUS. RIGHT POSITION

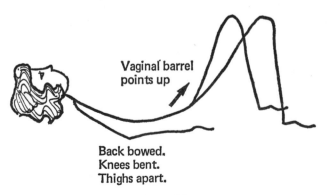

Vaginal barrel
points up

Back bowed.
Knees bent.
Thighs apart.

Figure 11.

active part in insertion, adopting a position with the male lying flat on has back and his partner squatting over him and inserting from the superior position. This gives control of speed and timing of the procedure to the woman and makes sure that in taking the active part, she is continuing the process learned in the treatment sessions. At some stage before this time, it is important to discuss with the husband the nature of the problem and to obtain his co-operation in the early attempts at full intercourse, recognizing that plenty of lubrication must be used and adequate contraception must be ensured if there is any need for fear on the woman's part to avoid pregnancy.

Chapter 8

SEXUAL PROBLEMS IN THE HANDICAPPED

IF AN UNDERSTANDING of the needs and behaviour patterns of society has been slow to emerge from the Dark Ages of sexual repression, how much more have the problems of the handicapped in this respect been misunderstood and ignored? Handicap may occur in the previously healthy as a result of trauma or disease. Handicap may be present at birth, from maldevelopment or from pre– and peri-natal influences. Handicap may be physical, affecting the function of limbs or the autonomic system, or it may derive from disabilities of the special senses, in particular blindness or deafness. Handicap may be mental and affect intelligence or emotional stability.

Such individuals, however, are as likely as the rest of society to have sexual needs which require expression from time to time if such a person is to be able to lead a full life. The handicapped unfortunately suffer from disabilities which society imposes upon them in addition to those of their basic problem.

The individual who is handicapped from birth is less likely to be able to benefit from such educational facilities as exist at present and is less liable to obtain the experience in adolescence which the non-handicapped enjoy. The handicapped are to some extent shunned and feared, and their attractiveness to others may be diminished. They may well have, as a result, built-in inferiority feelings which in sexual terms may force them to remain fixated at an immature level. They can then become prey to the unscrupulous.

Non-handicapped people find it difficult to relate to the

handicapped. They are not sure how the latter will respond or what their capabilities are. Embarrassment may be present. Normal levels of social intercourse therefore may be restricted. For example, individuals often avoid taking the hand of someone who is sitting in a wheelchair. The amount of non-sexual fondling from adults and from their peer group in adolescence is diminished for the same reason. Yet such people often need more physical contact and reassurance that they are potentially lovable than do the non-handicapped. Physical contact is one of the ways in which we affirm ourselves as potentially lovable. The adolescent who suffers such deprivation is likely to be less sure of himself or herself when making an approach to others.

Furthermore, considerable amounts of time may be spent in communal environments where the opportunity for the normal amount of adolescent exchange of ideas and sexual exploration may not come their way because of the lack of privacy. Such behaviour may be frowned upon by staff who see it as a threat to the smooth running of the establishment and may fear criticism from others if it is allowed. Few such institutions provide privacy or even a place where adults who are hospitalized may meet their legitimate partners and relate to each other at a sexual level without fear of interruption.

As Haslam has pointed out (Haslam, 1976), the blind present particularly complex problems. When meeting a blind child, a sighted person may allow him to run his hand over their face. It is a way of letting the blind gain a sense of seeing the other. How is the blind child, however, to be taught the differences between the sexes and about human sexuality? The blind learn most by touching. Blind adolescents are in this sense cheated in that they cannot even engage in the individual kind of normal sex play that children of this age-group normally obtain. Because they cannot see, they do not even know when they are alone. In the female, there is the additional problem with regard to menstruation, where the blind adolescent may suffer acute embarrassment if she misses the visual awareness that menstruation has commenced.

The more severely physically handicapped such as those who

are spastic or have degrees of paraplegia may still be of normal intelligence and able to appreciate normal sexual desire although
their ability to function normally in sexual circumstances may
be impaired. At a less severe level, some may require assistance
to get into a sexual position with their partner, and if both are
handicapped, may require the help of a non-handicapped individual to enable intercourse to take place. The more severely
handicapped may not even be able to induce orgasm through un-
aided masturbatory efforts, yet orgasmic release may be an important part of their needs, the denial of which may lead to much
unhappiness and frustration. Society can only solve such problems through caring and understanding and the realization that
some individuals may need guidance as to alternative forms of
sexual expression. For some, intercourse may never be possible,
but a sensitive partner or the use of sexual aids may allow them
in some cases to achieve at least some level of fulfillment, imper-
fect though this may be compared with their non-handicapped
fellow human beings.

The mentally handicapped also have difficulties. Many have
been confined to an institutional existence for much of their
lives, where the sexes have been until recent times segregated
but where, at the same time, homosexual contact or overt masturbation has been discouraged. Sexual development and sexual drive, however, can be normal in such individuals, but the
fact that they are less articulate has meant that they could offer
little protest. Indeed, their sexual education having been minimal, many are unable to understand what motivates their behaviour. The more handicapped may show less inhibition about
the public display of sexual behaviour or of the genitalia than
does the general population with a higher degree of social
awareness.

Should normals allow subnormals to enjoy the same freedom
of sexual expression? Put in this way, public attitudes may
sound arrogant and presumptuous, but we must not forget that
sexual promiscuity has been a reason for admission to subnormality hospitals in the past. For example, prior to the 1959
Mental Health Act in Great Britain, a legal category of patient

existed known as "moral imbecile." Some patients perhaps now classified as inadequate personalities have been detained in hospitals for many years because society was unable to prevent them from mating indiscriminately and, in the case of females, getting pregnant thereby.

There are, of course, arguments on both sides. Those who run hospitals for the mentally retarded are concerned that no one should think they are encouraging immorality. Indeed, in Great Britain, for individuals of normal I.Q. on the staff of such hospitals to have a sexual relationship with a patient is a criminal offence. (Indeed under the 1959 Mental Health Act in Great Britain, it is similarly a criminal offence for a member of the staff to have a sexual relationship on such premises with a patient receiving treatment for a psychiatric illness.) Nevertheless, it seems inappropriate in residential hospitals that all sexual activity available to the rest of the population should be automatically denied to those who, through no fault of their own, have this affliction.

A further problem for the staff of such hospitals, however, lies in the sensitivities of relatives who see the staff in the role of being *in loco parentis* even when such patients are adult.

Finally, there is the question as to whether such individuals should be allowed to sire or bear children. Some causes of mental retardation are inheritable, but there are nevertheless many patients in mental retardation units where the cause of the subnormality is not inherited and the child would in all probability be born with normal intelligence. Nevertheless, the subnormal might well be unable to bring up such a child adequately, and pregnancy is therefore undesirable.

It is possible to guard against these contingencies by administering a contraceptive pill or by sterilization. Can the mentally retarded individual, however, give valid consent to such procedures, and is it ethical for relatives to give consent on a subnormal individual's behalf? These are ethical matters which society must regulate. Whatever the logic of the argument, it is the collective emotion of society which is likely to be the main determinant of policy.

Those individuals who develop a handicap when already mature may at least be able to discover some way of compensating for their loss. It is the secondarily handicapped who are more likely to attend for psychosexual counselling when a physical handicap has made sexual activity difficult for the couple and is denying both the handicapped and the non-handicapped partner the means towards sexual fulfillment.

Such people may need practical advice on the ways their handicap can be overcome and how other means may be found of stimulating or being stimulated and of conveying their love for each other in a physical form that both can accept. Couples may need, as it were, official permission to act sexually in ways they may have previously thought of as outside the normal range or mildly deviant. This is true of much counselling. Many couples retain the idea that for sexual expression to be in some way legitimate, it should be potentially procreative; they feel that eroticism developed in a non-procreative manner when heterosexual intercourse is not the aim nor the end is in some way immoral. This no doubt reflects religiously biased Victorian standards of morality. This type of attitude has done much to create the stigma born by those who enjoy eroticism of a non-heterosexual nature, be it homosexual, transvestite or, as contemporary society might call it, deviant, and must have added enormously to the unnecessary guilt and shame forced upon this section of the population because of disapproval of otherwise totally harmless activities.

Thus for the handicapped, conventional heterosexual intercourse may prove painful or indeed impossible. The use of oral sex and mutual masturbation or the addition of sexual aids to the couple's armamentarium may be something they had not previously considered. If they can be allowed to accept at an emotional level that such alternatives are a means towards the continuing expression of love between them, then their sexual lives may continue even though the previous behaviour patterns must needs be altered.

Secondary handicap may affect sexual performance in a wide variety of ways. Direct trauma to the genitalia is fortunately rare outside of wartime conditions. Degenerative disease as a result of peripheral autonomic neuropathy may arise from diabetes, pernicious anaemia, hypertension and excessive use of nicotine. There are many other rarer causes: Neurological disease such as disseminated sclerosis and other generalized disturbances of the central nervous system can produce the same effect. Rheumatic conditions present problems through the pain produced by movement associated with sexual activity and by limitation of joint motility. Spasticity presents particular problems. Local disease such as neoplasia, the effects of operative interference on the prostate, or abdominal operations producing colostomy or ileostomy may affect sexual function. Cardio-vascular and pulmonary disease may limit the amount of exertion that can be tolerated. Spinal cord lesions may affect erective ability or ejaculatory function along with disturbances of bowel and bladder function.

Finally, drugs which may be prescribed for patients for the treatment of other conditions may interfere with arousal or ejaculatory competence. Of particular concern here are the hypotensive drugs, hormone preparations including the contraceptive pill, phenothiazines which cause hyperprolactinaemia by suppressing dopamine levels and anti-depressants of both tricyclic and mono-amine oxidase inhibitor groups.

Pain may be controlled by the use of analgesics or anti-inflammatory agents, particularly if the dosage is timed so that the maximal effect coincides with planned sexual activity. Narcotics and tranquillizers can, of course, also produce an adverse effect. Steroids used in the treatment of many collagenoses may have implications on sexual function and can decrease libido and cause testicular atrophy and impotence.

Some cerebral dysfunctions are associated with vascular, traumatic, neoplastic or degenerative disorders. Those which induce temporal lobe disturbances may affect sexual function both by inducing impulsive and inappropriate sexual behaviour or, on the other hand, by decreasing libido. Both conditions respond favourably to drugs now available for the treatment of temporal lobe epileptic states.

Spasticity related to upper motor neurone lesions may be severe enough to interfere with vaginal penetration or containment. The use of benzodiazepines may be sufficient to control this. In severer cases, injection of phenol into the motor endplate regions of the spastic muscles or into the peripheral nerves innovating these muscles can be tried.

Ejaculation is often a problem in spinal cord lesions. Penile stimulation with a vibrator or the installation of intra-vaginal and intra-rectal electrical stimulation have all been tried. But since ejaculation is often retrograde, sperm may need to be collected from the bladder if fertility is the main problem. The spermicidal effects of the urine can be minimized by alkalinizing it with sodium bicarbonate taken orally for several days beforehand. (Crown, S. 1976)

Patients with cardio-vascular or pulmonary disease may require assessment of physical capacity through monitored exercise procedures and continuous electro-cardiographic recording and measurements of pulse and blood pressure.

Colostomy and ileostomy present particular problems for the individual and the partner. The cosmetic effect may be inhibitory to the partner or indeed to the patient, who may feel that the partner will find him unattractive after this type of mutilatory operation. Apart from this, colostomy should have few other effects; but ileostomy not uncommonly induces impotence or frigidity as a result of nerves crucial to sexual function being divided as part of the total operative procedure.

Surgical procedures may be useful in assisting to restore some degree of sexual function in a number of ways. The use of prosthetic implants has already been considered. Spasticity of lower limb muscles may be reduced by an anterior rhizotomy or other neuro-surgical techniques. Incontinence accompanying the neuropathic bladder may be an indication for an ileal loop procedure or the surgical implantation of a pneumatic artificial urethral sphincter. Corrective surgery is allegedly effective in impotence associated with arterial occlusive disease such as the Leriche's syndrome.

In summary, therefore, the therapist who is consulted by the handicapped patient must use or have access to a wide variety of skills. Educational counselling is of vital importance in the young and those with primary handicaps. Education of society can also be stimulated if the professions take a lead in such matters. For the secondarily handicapped, the therapist must be aware of the possibilities open to handicapped individuals in terms of alternative techniques and the use of sexual aids. He must also be able to advise on the use of drugs to alleviate some symptoms and equally on which drugs can themselves inhibit sexual performance.

He must be able to assess when a handicap in a patient is the cause of the sexual dysfunction and when it is a coincidental finding. This may apply in such conditions as diabetes, where the coincidental finding of impotence may imply the presence of a peripheral neuropathy and an autonomic neuropathy which has diminished sexual arousal. Equally, he must assess when the diabetes is of no relevance and the impotence is induced by other causes, perhaps a secondary anxiety. This type of problem is also important in post-traumatic disturbances of sexual function where compensation may be an issue. A patient who claims that his impotence has been caused by a back injury, for example, but who shows no disturbance of bladder or bowel function, and whose abdominal and cremasteric reflexes are intact is more likely to be suffering from an anxiety-induced disability or malingering.

Finally, the therapist must be aware of the type of cases that can profitably be referred for surgical intervention and have a good system of liaison between the psychosexual clinic and the departments of genito-urinary surgery.

Section III

SEXUAL BEHAVIOURAL ANOMALIES

Chapter 9

INTRODUCTION

T HE THIRD SECTION of this book will be devoted to problems concerning homosexuality, gender identity and deviancy. We have grouped these problems under the general heading of sexual behavioural anomalies. As will be discussed in the chapters to follow, however, this grouping is for convenience and does not imply any direct connection either aetiologically or symptomatically. Indeed, many groups in society would deny the relevance of medicine or psychiatry in investigating the aspects of behaviour portrayed in the pages to follow.

The author hopes to show, however, that there is a legitimate area for study, if only that the doctor may be better able to help individuals with such behaviour problems who seek help by increasing his or her awareness of how such groups function in society, since empathy cannot come without understanding.

In terms of sexual dysfunctions, the problems included under a general heading of deviancy are widespread. Some are anti-social or illegal, such as paedophilia; others are conditioned patterns of behaviour, such as fetishism which are necessary to the individual's orgasmic functioning.

There seems little to be gained in following a descriptive pattern of entities merely of interest for their rarity or forensic bizarreness. Most deviant behaviour overlaps such boundaries since the participants are often driven by a search for novelty rather than sticking to descriptive boundaries.

It is logically doubtful whether transvestism should be part of a book on sexual problems at all, since the behaviour is a matter of gender identity in which sexuality is not as a rule distorted nor plays much of a part in the adopted behaviour patterns of crossdressing.

Homosexuality is certainly a distortion from a heterosexual norm, but so is red hair from a blonde-brunette continuum. This point will be argued in the relevant chapter.

Section III has been divided, therefore, into the following classificiation with general sub-divisions:

1. Homosexuality
2. Transvestism and allied problems
3. Deviancy
a. Paedophilia
b. Exhibitionism and voyeurism
c. Fetishism
d. Sado-masochism
e. Others

Sexual appetite is a natural function of human activities, indeed any animal's activities, and in the absence of the ability to make a satisfactory heterosexual union, the drive is displaced into other channels. Thus, the degree of emotional maturity an individual shows may be the main factor in the type of deviancy which develops. It should be noted, however that many deviant practices are only deviant if practised to the exclusion of normal heterosexual relationships. Many may be practised as occasional variants under particular circumstances by otherwise normal individuals for the sake of variety or in conditions where normal outlets are temporarily unavailable or as a prelude to normal intercourse, in order to titillate a tiring palate.

It should be further noted that the performance of deviant sexual behaviour, as indeed the performance of any other deviant behaviour, is basically of no concern to anyone other than the individual as long as no anti-social activity infringes or modifies in an undesirable way the thinking and activities of another individual. As will be noted in the final paragraphs of this review, the involvement of the law in the matter of deviancy takes little account of this principle, many of the laws still on the statute books being archaic in the extreme. In general, the medical practitioner may become involved in deviancy for two reasons. One is because the individual regrets his deviancy in much the same way an alcoholic may regret his excessive drinking and, while enjoying the experience, nevertheless would prefer to channel his drive into more normal routes. Under these circumstances he may be offered counselling in order to accept his disability or he may be treated in an attempt to remove it and convert his thinking into normal heterosexual directions. The other occasion for referral is through the courts, where an individual has fallen foul of the law appertaining to his deviation and may seek help or be referred unwillingly as a condition of probation. The desire to change may be minimal, the referral simply being to pacify the ruling group in society. Under these circumstances the doctor should be cautious of becoming involved in a treatment process which is probably doomed to failure from the outset.

Chapter 10

NORMS

WE SHALL BE CONCERNED at various points in this review with the problem of normality. This is relevant in terms of normal sexual response where, for example, orgasmic frequency may be the cause of concern to the patient, and more particularly when dealing with subjects under the broad heading of deviancy where patients or their partners may be concerned about whether patterns of behaviour are acceptable.

The concept of normality is concerned with the statistical average. Let us take height as an example. If the population of the world could each be measured and the results were to be added together and divided by the total number of persons measured, then the figure obtained would represent the mean of the height of the world population. Let us say that this came to 5 feet, 6 inches. This figure by itself would merely tell us the average height of humans but would not tell us the range. However, if all these measurements were plotted on a graph, then a curve of distribution could be obtained relating height to percentage of the population at any particular point on the graph. In practise, of course, this is done with samples of the population; for such a measure, a normal curve of distribution is found in Figure 12.

In practise, this normal curve would be skewed slightly at both ends, a small number of abnormally tall people would be found at one end, the result of a disease process producing excessive growth, while at the other end of the scale, the same would apply, where an abnormally short stature was again the result of some disease process affecting growth.

This normal curve of distribution could be further broken down usefully by distinguishing between male and female, since the average height would differ between the sexes. It could also be broken down into different racial groups, since the height of some populations is genetically determined as, for example, in the bushmen or pygmy races in Africa.

However it was broken down, a normal curve of distribution would still be found for the particular population studied; in statistical terms, two-thirds of the population would fall within one standard deviation (S.D.) on either side of this mean. A further one-sixth would fall outside of this range on the small side and a similar one-sixth on the tall side.

Exactly the same type of distribution curve would be found if we were to consider intelligence, weight, size of feet or any other measure where there are genetic and environmentally determined variations. One could draw the same type of curve for a table of orgasmic frequency per week or for size of genitalia

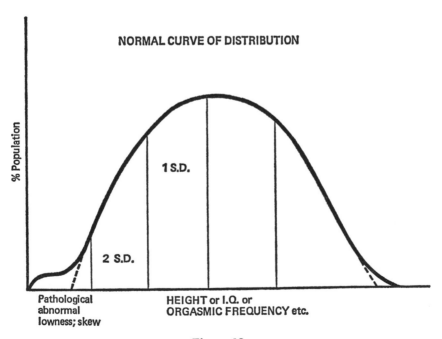

Figure 12.

and so on.

What therefore is normal? The majority of people do not fall exactly on the mean. They are a little above or below it. Are those who are outside one standard deviation from the mean to be considered abnormal? In other words, is someone who is 6 feet, 2 inches tall abnormal or is someone whose I.Q. is 75 abnormal? One can say that they are outside of the range of normal only when they fall outside the normal curve of distribution. Equally, one can say that they deviate further from the mean than the majority of the population even if they remain within the normal curve but are at either end of it. But these are statistical concepts, and we are not implying a pathological condition unless the individual is at this extreme as a result of some congenital or acquired disability or disease process.

If one applies this concept to sexual identification, taking heterosexual mating as the norm, then it will be seen that homosexuality is a qualitatively different phenomenon which cannot be plotted on a range of distribution of heterosexual behaviour. Thus, in this statistical sense such behaviour is abnormal.

On the other hand, if one were to take a group of fourteen-years-olds, it would be found that masturbation was the norm of sexual behaviour, and a normal curve of distribution of masturbation rate could be plotted. Heterosexuality would be qualitatively different and statistically abnormal.

The point to be made is that one cannot plot homosexuality, heterosexuality and masturbation all on the same graph and get a normal curve of distribution.

If, as Kinsey has done, sexuality is considered in one dimension with total homosexual commitment at one end of a continuum and total heterosexuality at the other, with bisexuality coming midway along this line, then a normal curve of distribution would not be found. Two curves would be found, as shown in Figure 13, a larger one at the heterosexual end with a smaller peak at the homosexual end, the intervening space showing a trough.

We will take this point up further when considering homosexuality specifically. The same argument can apply to any aspect of behaviour which is considered outside the statistical norm and in that sense deviant. If one thinks logically and removes emotive conditioning from one's argument, then such deviation should not be considered in any different light from that of the individual who is 6 feet, 2 inches or 4 feet, 8 inches tall. They may be different from the rest of us, but neither the genius nor the simpleton should be condemned but rather understood and accepted for themselves as people.

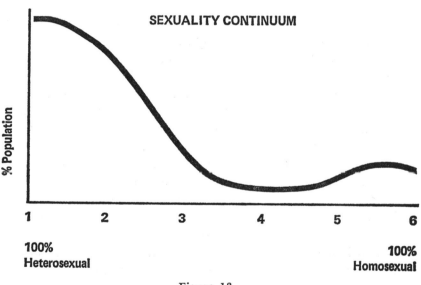

Figure 13.

Chapter 11

HOMOSEXUALITY

THAT GROUP OF PEOPLE in whom sexual interest lies in their own sex rather than in the opposite sex form a sizable minority of the population. Much misunderstanding surrounds this whole topic, and it is the subject of considerable prejudice. Some societies accept homosexual behaviour as a normal variant, and there is complete tolerance with regard to whether sexual expression is heterosexual or homosexual. Some societies have tried to separate physical love from mental or emotional love and have extolled the latter while regarding the former as pernicious. This has applied both to homosexual and heterosexual activity.

Some religious groups have treated homosexual behaviour as sinful, and ecclesiastical law and indeed most religious movements popular in the West from mediaeval to Victorian times, including Christian, Muslim and Judaic law, have prescribed various penalties, sometimes severe, for activity outside the accepted normal practice of the times.

Secular law in countries based upon English law have also at times produced absurdly severe penalties for what to the majority of unprejudiced thinkers must be fairly harmless pieces of eroticism.

Often only particular types of homosexual behaviour have been the subject of legal prohibition. Thus, in Britain female homosexuality has never been illegal. Some homosexual behaviour is tied to the laws governing soliciting and importuning, while some laws relate specifically to anal intercourse. This latter is legal in Britain at present between consenting male adults in private but not between a male and a female even if married.

In those countries and states where homosexual behaviour is legal, there are often age limits set. Thus, sexual activity between two males in Britain remains illegal if one or both are under the age of twenty-one, whereas sexual behaviour between male and female can occur from sixteen onwards. These laws seemingly ignore the fact that homosexual behaviour is a normal pattern seen in adolescence in a large percentage of both the male and female population. This has been shown by community surveys such as the one carried out by Kinsey. The majority of the adolescent population passes through this phase and into heterosexual activity, and there is no evidence to suggest that experimental homosexual behaviour during the early teens creates any kind of later predisposition or pattern.

Indeed, if one is to consider homosexuality as part of a continuum of normal sexual behaviour, then it is probably more common in the early teens than heterosexuality is. Furthermore, auto-sexuality or masturbation is commonest of all; if one were to argue, therefore, on the bases of percentages, it would be more logical in this age-group to consider heterosexuality as deviant.

An argument that continues to rage between the more orthodox side of the medical profession, the law and the church on the one hand and the representatives of homophile organizations such as the Campaign for Homosexual Equality and the various "gay lib" movements on the other is concerned with whether homosexual behaviour should be considered as an example of perverted sexuality or as one end of a continuum, albeit the minority end, of total sexual experience.

The work of Kinsey has shown that some 30 percent of adults have engaged in homosexual activity involving the physical expression of feelings leading to orgasm. Furthermore, some 10 percent of the population are permanently committed to homosexual behaviour patterns. Kinsey has further shown that bisexuality, where sexual expression may occur in both heterosexual and homosexual forms at different times, is by no means uncommon. The incidence of homosexual behaviour increases where there is absence of a heterosexual outlet. This occurs in institutions, prisons and any areas where one sex is segregated for any length of time. Thus, homosexuality is not an all-or-none thing any more than is heterosexuality.

The incidence of homosexuality approximates the incidence of redheads in the community. This is not to imply any connection between the two but merely to point out that to have red hair as opposed to black or blonde is a minority variant outside of the individual's control and associated in some people's minds with particular personality characteristics. Fortunately, nobody has as yet suggested that all redheads be locked up if they talk to each other or that they have their hair colour compulsorily changed by dying to black or blonde.

Homosexuality should not be thought of as an homogenous entity. It seems likely that a percentage of cases are prenatally determined either through genetic factors or through influences on the foetus or hormone changes in the mother at critical times in the pregnancy. The fact that research into such problems remains inconclusive may well reflect that the cases studied indiscriminately included not only those in the genetic or prenatal category, but also those who show homosexual behaviour patterns as a result of environmentally determined conditioning events that have occurred in childhood or adolescence and those in whom heterophobia is the main aetiological factor.

The same problem occurs in researching the causes of such conditions as depression, rheumatic diseases or alcoholism, where particular symptom complexes may be the end result of a wide variety of differing aetiologies.

Should the medical profession and psychiatry in particular involve itself at all, therefore, in the consideration of social behaviour patterns in humans? To answer this question it is possible to revert to our example of red hair. Perhaps medicine should concern itself with homosexuality to the same extent that it concerns itself with redheads; no more, no less.

To elaborate on this, it is legitimate research to try to determine why one person's hair is one colour while another's is different. It is equally legitimate to consider the causes of baldness and to try to treat this problem. Furthermore, redheads are as likely to develop baldness problems as are blondes or brunettes.

It is conceivable, however, to consider a situation where redheads might be less or more prone to baldness than blondes or brunettes; again this would be a legitimate area of research and therapy. Furthermore, if being redheaded had some selective disadvantage to the group in terms of their social functioning or society's attitudes, then such a group might be more likely to seek help and advice and would therefore merit it, though it is arguable whether, if there were a treatment that converted redheadedness to blonde on a permanent basis, it should be applied simply because society preferred blondes. Better perhaps that the profession be engaged in assisting in the education of society that redheads are just as nice.

Such an argument could equally be applied to the colour of skin. In terms of sexuality, therefore, we can say that the types and causes of sexual activity are a legitimate area of research. Homosexuality as a phenomenon is a legitimate area of study. Homosexuals as a group in our society are liable to be more stressed than the rest of the population for social reasons and are at a selective disadvantage related to the family patterns of our culture. They are likely, therefore, to require help more frequently and should be offered it. They should be offered help, however, on the basis of their complaints and not simply on the basis that their sexual orientation is different from the majority.

This argument is legitimate only insofar as homosexuality can be considered as one end of a continuum and a normal variant of behaviour, i.e. directly comparable with redheadedness. To the extent that it is viewed as a distorted pattern of behaviour that produces certain disadvantages to the individual and for which there is a definable pre- or post-natal aetiology, then it would be legitimate to seek to prevent its occurrence and to attempt to treat it in the sense of establishing heterosexual behaviour patterns in those who request treatment, though not of course in those who do not wish it. These two conflicting points of view seem at present to be irreconcilable, but in the absence of a defined post-natal aetiology and the absence of any genuinely effective long-term treatment, then it seems more appropriate to the author to adopt the former point of view.

Let us consider, therefore, a classification of homosexuality along the lines we have discussed:

ADOLESCENTS. Homosexuality is a normal developmental phase of no consequence in a large proportion of individuals in this age-group.

TRUE HOMOSEXUALS. In this group, most of whom are reasonably contented in their role, there is likely to be some pre-natal cause. Members of this group are stable and capable of making mature adult relationships, and apart from their sexual orientation, have no other distinguishing feature from the general population. In a tolerant society, they are unlikely to seek help for homosexuality per se.

EFFEMINATE HOMOSEXUALS. Research suggests that homosexuality is present in some 10 percent of the population. Transvestism in its various forms has been estimated as between 1 and 0.1 percent of the population. It thus seems probable that in approximately 1 in 1,000, the two might coincide. The great bulk of transvestites, as will be shown in a subsequent chapter, are heterosexual in their sexual orientation, but the combination of the two may offer a simple explanation for the presence of the "drag queens" who enjoy adopting feminine attributes and taking a submissive role in sexual activity with other males. Transvestites are not popular with the bulk of homosexuals, who are non-effeminate in their general interests.

BISEXUALS. Kinsey has shown that many people are capable of both homosexual and heterosexual activity at different times and are able to obtain gratification in both roles. For the well-adjusted individual this presents no particular problem, but younger people are quite likely to attend the clinic after a homosexual experience that they have found at the time enjoyable but has later created anxiety if they believe that it implies a full-time state of homosexuality in later life, which they may not wish. Such individuals can usually be reassured.

HETEROPHOBES. In this group the problem lies in the failure of the individual to relate sexually to the opposite sex. Libido is thus channelled into a homosexual route for secondary reasons. Such people should be accessible to psychotherapy or behaviour therapy intervention.

"Loo-Lurkers." In this group, again, homosexuality is not very strictly of relevance. We have coined this term to describe individuals who indulge in genitally orientated mutual masturbatory activity, which is basically an extension of narcissistic behaviour in which the sex of the partner, who is often anonymous, is of little relevance. Such meetings often take place in public toilets, and since the problem usually afflicts the male, the sex of the partner is determined by this. Such individuals see this type of activity as being less threatening because no relationship develops. The sex of the partner, however, is a matter of convenience.

Paedophiliac Homosexuals. This last category is included here for completeness but will be discussed in the chapter on deviancy. Such individuals are attracted to young children because they are often sexually less potent with adults and feel inadequate. The activity may be homosexual or heterosexual, depending on circumstances.

Incidence

Little factual detail is available as to the general incidence of sexual deviation in the community. This is because well-adjusted deviants are unlikely to come the way of the medical practitioner. Kinsey's survey in the United States, however, has contributed considerably to the study of this problem, at any rate in western society, though cultural differences cause considerable variation in different cultures. Perhaps Kinsey's main contribution has been in pointing out the normality, in terms of the percentage of the population involved, of many practices which in the past have been considered as abnormal and have thus created guilt on the part of their participants, usually unnecessarily.

Kinsey states that in the American male population, single and married between adolescence and old age, 24 percent of the total sexual outlet is derived from solitary sources, that is to say masturbation and dream orgasm. Heterosexual sources, petting and coitus, account for 69.4 percent, and 6.3 percent of the total number of orgasms are derived from homosexual contacts in their series. Relations with other species amounted to 0.5 percent of the total outlet. Kinsey, however, draws attention to the concept of bisexuality and the rating of individuals on a scale from complete heterosexuality to complete homosexuality. In his series, at least 37 percent of the male population had had some homosexual experience between the beginning of adolescence and old age, many of these being single contacts or contacts between adolescents of an exploratory nature. Among those who remain unmarried until the age of thirty-five, 50 percent have had homosexual experience. The percentage is considerably higher in situations where heterosexual behaviour is prohibited, such as mental and/or criminal institutions.

Kinsey's survey of 1948, in an investigation of over 4,000 males and females, showed that some 4 percent of white males were exclusively homosexual all their lives and that more than one-third admitted to at least some adult homosexual experience, the criterion being contact with another male leading to orgasm. They introduced a rating scale of homosexuality, giving a maximum of 6 points to those who had orgasm only with other men and 0 to men who had orgasm only with women. A mid-score indicated those who had orgasm equally with either sex. They found that there were more men with intermediate scores than with a maximum of 6, so that partial homosexuals were more common than complete inverts. Nearly one-fourth of all men had indulged in some homosexual activity, and 10 percent were exclusively homosexual for a period of at least three consecutive years.

Publication of Kinsey's second report in 1953 showed that active lesbianism or female homosexuality is less common than male homosexuality. A sample of 6,000 white women showed that only 13 percent had had homosexual contact to orgasm by the age of forty-five and only 4 percent remained exclusively homosexual throughout their lives.

Homosexuality does not appear to relate significantly to physique, although some homosexuals adopt female patterns of behaviour and dress and may adopt female mannerisms in order to encourage acceptance by a male partner. In fact, however, the majority of individuals with homosexual inclinations in all other ways appear and act normal for their sexual identity. Attempts have been made through psychological testing to identify homosexual individuals; male-female indices are identified, for example, in the Minnesota Multiphasic Personality Inventory. Usually, homosexuals cannot be divided into active and passive categories, since the majority tend to adopt each role at different points in time. Again, however, as homosexuality is probably not an homogenous diagnostic category, it may well be that certain sub-groups can be identified where the aetiology is particularly likely to produce one feature or another. Homosexuals, in general, do not identify themselves with the opposite sex; the condition is quite distinct from transsexualism and transvestism, though the conditions may coexist.

Relatively less study has been made concerning female homosexuality, with few published studies being based on representative samples of the lesbian population. Kenyon (1968), however, has done such a controlled study, obtaining his cases from an organization devoted to lesbian interests that was willing to co-operate in research. In the beginning of his study he reviews the present literature, and in a later section the social and psychiatric aspects. Kenyon found that 21 percent had poor relationships with their mothers, and 35 percent of the mothers had died at the time of the study. Equally, there was a history of poor relationships with the fathers. Their parents' marriage was rated as unsatisfactory by 64 percent, and there was a higher incidence of separation and divorce than in the control group. A positive psychiatric history occurred more frequently in the mothers, and a family history of homosexuality was found in 24 percent.

One of the reasons that female homosexuality has a lower incidence than male homosexuality may be that in the male, ready expression may be given to the physical acting out of homosexual feelings, whereas in the female this takes on a more romantic non-physical form. Davis (1929) in a study of 1,200 unmarried women graduates, noted that 50 percent had had intense emotional relationships with other women, which in two-thirds of the cases did not give rise to any physical expression.

Particular problems are faced by individuals with homosexual interests due to rather stringent legal prohibitions, which will be discussed in the final paragraphs. Ethical and religious issues are also involved, and Christian dogma has long considered homosexual behaviour in all circumstances immoral and inexcusable. Doctor Geoffrey Fisher, Archbishop of Canterbury, declared in 1953: "Let it be understood that homosexual indulgence is a shameful vice and a grievous sin from which deliverance is to be sought by every means." (D.J. West, 1976)

There has, however, in recent years been a tendency towards more understanding of such problems, and this has led to some liberalization of the law. Social intolerance, however, remains marked in western countries, though in many Arab and Asian countries, where homosexual practices are commonplace and regarded by most people with easygoing indifference, no great trouble arises. It is interesting that homosexuals plead for understanding as a minority; they attempt to obtain this understanding by emphasizing their normal aspects in contrast to other minority groups, to which they show intolerance equal to that shown them. Thus, West identifies the means by which homosexuals may meet discreetly and mentions the guides and directories, in particular the Grey Guide and the Lavender Baedeker, which list country-by-country the bars and hotels where homosexuals may expect to find tolerance. He emphasizes the normality of the majority of homosexuals in dress and speech, but goes on to say, "Some may arrive looking like grotesque caricatures of women or actually in drag, i.e. in female dress, swishing about demonstratively and advertising their presence." He also states, "The butch types who swagger along in men's trousers and cropped hair . . . parody the normal male as grotesquely as the mincing, dyed and powdered queens parody the normal woman."

In fact, there is now a wide variety of clubs and societies and magazines catering to those with homosexual inclination. With a change of the law in Britain and in some American states to allow homosexual activity between consenting adults in private, requests for treatment from the psychological services have considerably dwindled.

Aetiology

It must be appreciated that in such an heterogenous group, the aetiology is likely to be diverse; any attempt to lump all such individuals together and seek a common cause is likely to be doomed to failure. In searching for possible causes of homosexuality therefore, it is important to disregard those groups besides true homosexuals and possibly effeminate homosexuals as listed earlier. The aetiology of transvestism will be considered in another chapter, as will the deviancy to which heterophobes and loo-lurkers more properly belong.

Patients with heterophobia can usually trace their problem to early environmental causes, for which analytically orientated psychotherapy may be most appropriate.

Gadpaille (1972) presents a useful review of the aetiology and psycho-dynamics of homosexuality with ninety-seven further references. He states that many of the early figures in modern psychiatry such as Havelock Ellis, Krafft-Ebing and others considered homosexuality to be of constitutional or hereditary origin. With the development of increasing understanding of psycho-dynamics following Freud, most thinking has shifted to the importance of conflicts in psychosexual development within the context of emotionally important experiences and relationships during childhood and adolescence: "The wish for sexual gratification with the mother becomes transformed into the wish to enjoy it in the same manner as the mother does. . . the father becomes the object of love and the individual strives to submit himself to him as the mother does in a passive, receptive manner" (Fenichel, 1945). This is determined by a previous fixation at the anal erotic stage.

The second theory of homosexual development is essentially an interpersonal one that evolved from the researches of Bieber and his associates, who found the typical family constellation in the background of male homosexuals consisting of a close-binding, intimate mother and a detached or indifferent hostile father. The mother's influence demasculinized the son and stripped the father of admirable masculine qualities, while the father made identification with himself unpalatable (Bieber, 1962).

Evidence for the inheritance of perversion comes from the work of Lang on intersex in nature, Kallmann's twin studies and genetic studies by Slater, who noted that perverts come low in the sibship order statistically, comparing this with Down's syndrome, those at the bottom of the pecking order tending to be homosexual and the youngest in family likely to be the lowest in the pecking order.

Harlow and Harlow (1962), working on the consequences of rearing conditions to rhesus monkeys, have uniformly demonstrated that inadequate mothering and lack of peer group social contact and sex play during childhood later produces adults who totally lack the capacity for adult sexual behaviour, successful copulation and parental function. There was clear evidence that peer group social and sexual play was more important than mothering, since lack of mothering in this respect could be overcome by peer experience, but lack of peer experience left ineradicable incapacities. While none of the males recovered, some of the females paired with experienced males became receptive and conceived and gave birth. Subsequently, however, they became totally rejecting mothers.

Kollar et al. (1968) showed that the same ineptness in the display of adult sexual responses is found in chimpanzees reared in isolation until past maturity, which indicates the critical period for learning adult sexuality to be between puberty and early adulthood.

Turning to neuro-endocrine and neuro-anatomical studies, it has been shown that the anterior hypothalamus governs and regulates the physiological aspects of reproductive function and sexual behaviour (Harris, 1964). Harris reviews the literature and reports his own experiments demonstrating that neuro-humoral substances elaborated in the anterior hypothalamus are carried by portal vessels in the pituitary stalk and in turn regulate release of anterior hypophyseal gonadotrophins. There appears to be a nodal point for penile erection in the medial portion of the medial dorsal thalamic nucleus.

There are interesting proximities between sexual and other functions. Thus, the limbic lobe is bent around upon itself, bringing into anatomic juxtaposition areas relating to oral, olfactory and ano-genital functions. This is not merely a physical proximity, but both oral and genital activity can be elicited together in identical discreet loci. Excitation in a region involved in oral mechanisms readily spills over into others concerned with genital function. Roeder (1970) has reported on electro-coagulation of Cajal's nucleus in the ventro-medial part of the hypothalamus as a treatment for criminal homosexuality.

Hormonal studies have shown that nature's prime disposition is to produce femaleness, maleness resulting from added androgen. Use of anti-androgen cyproterone acetate, a substance which blocks androgens, when injected into pregnant rats produces genetic male offspring with external genitalia identical to those of females. Thus, in the absence of androgen, morphology develops according to the female pattern without regard to the genotype of the animal (Neumann and Elger, 1966). If male hormones are given to pregnant rats early in pregnancy, then female offspring are more assertive. Perloff (1965) states that no endocrine factor is found in homosexuality. Ryrie and Brown (1970) suggest, however, that there may be endocrine changes and refer to Loraine's work on testosterone differences in Edinburgh. Urinary testosterone levels were found to be abnormally low in exclusive homosexuals, and testosterone was raised in lesbians. Dewhurst (1969), however, found no relationship between sexual activity and steroid excretion patterns.

It seems that foetal hormones have an inductive or organizing effect upon the hypothalamus and that the absence of the androgenic effect at a particular critical period for a given species results in a brain organized to produce morphologic females. The presence of androgenic effect suppresses female morphology in favour of male morphology and organizes the hypothalamus to function acyclically in contrast to the cyclic function of the female pituitary gonadotrophin release pattern. Human studies on sexual function in Turner's syndrome, the adreno-genital syndrome and Kleinefelter's syndrome may have relevance.

The situation regarding hormones in the aetiology of homosexuality is a complex one. Giving oestrogens to females does not increase sexual desire but merely produces menorrhagia. Giving oestrogen to adults reduces sexual desire and causes feminizing in the male but does not alter the sexual or gender orientation of either the male or the female.

When androgens are taken by sexually normal females, they may experience some masculinizing changes and an increase in sexual desire, but they do not change the direction of sexual interests. Similarly, in the male, an enhancement of sexual desire may temporarily take place with increased vascularity and sensitivity of the penis, but again no change in sexual orientation is caused by giving such hormones to male homosexuals.

As West points out (1955), however, the possibility that deviant sexual behaviour in humans is caused by some glandular deficiency cannot be dismissed out of hand. The fact that upbringing and early experience have a powerful effect upon gender identity and sexual preference by no means rules out simultaneous operation of physical causes. Variations in physical constitution may render some individuals particularly vulnerable to environmental pressures.

Most of the older work on androgen levels in males yielded no convincing differences between homosexuals and heterosexuals. In recent years, however, more accurate methods of estimation have allowed some researchers to report significant differences. The male hormone testosterone can be measured, more particularly the breakdown products of 5-hydroxy-keto-steroids, namely androsterone and etiocholanolone. It has been shown that abnormally low urinary testosterone levels are found in some exclusively homosexual individuals. West also quotes research which has shown unusually high levels of testosterone in lesbians where oestrogen levels were also lowered.

The ratio of androsterone to etiocholanolone is characteristically much lower in women than in men. Research has shown that homosexuals had consistently lowered ratios compared with heterosexual males. Low ratios were also found in heterosexual males suffering from a variety of other abnormal conditions including depression and diabetes. This tendency was especially marked among those who were exclusively homosexual. The difference was not associated with lack of sexual activity on the part of the homosexual group, since they reported a frequency of sexual activity similar to that of the heterosexual controls. Although the mean ratios differed significantly, the range of individual variation was considerable. The amount of overlap between the two populations was too great to enable a competent identification of homosexuality or heterosexuality in a particular individual from his androsterone:etiocholanolone ratio alone. This difference is not clearly found in bisexual individuals.

In a further research study, those with Kinsey ratings of 5 or 6 were shown to have a significant lowering of sperm count and a reduction in sperm motility. This suggests some deficiency of hormone function, even though such individuals appear physically normal and seemingly virile.

The cause of such differences is of some interest. It must be noted that the hypothalamic region of the brain functions differently in males than in females. The male hypothalamus lacks the characteristic rhythmic activity that, through its influence upon the release of pituitary hormones, sets the pace for the female menstrual cycle. This part of the brain is also concerned with regulation of emotional reactions and aggressive responses; it seems possible that male and female styles of behaviour are differently programmed from birth by a distinctive neurological constitution of the hypothalamus.

An interesting area of research, therefore, is into how these brain centres become functionally differentiated into male and female patterns. There appears to be a critical phase of development when the hypothalamus becomes temporarily very sensitive to the level of circulating androgens. During this phase, a brief exposure to androgens suppresses the rhythmic activity upon which the female hormone cycle depends, so that even though an animal has the genetic endowment of a female, she will not as an adult display the periodic phases of a normal female. Similarly, lack of androgens at this time ensures that the rhythmic feminine brain characteristics develop in spite of an animal being genetically male.

The sensitivity of the brain to the type of hormone and the

concentration of hormone to which it will respond is permanently established at this time. Artificial manipulation of the hormone levels during this critical phase has been shown to have considerable effect upon subsequent adult behaviour. Small doses of androgens given to female rats at the critical time will permanently abolish the cyclical variation of hormone levels characteristic of the normal female. Upon reaching sexual maturity, the female rats' behaviour is affected by failing to display the usual receptive position in the presence of males and does not do so even when given artificially large doses of female hormone at this stage. Similarly, when given doses of androgens as an adult, she can be induced to perform mounting and male copulatory motions in spite of the absence of male genitalia. This does not occur in normal female rats whose brains have not been sensitized to androgens.

Furthermore, if male rats are castrated at a critical time and given doses of female hormone, a complete reversal of sexual behaviour can be produced so that the animals attempt to mate by presenting themselves to other males instead of mounting females. The temporary lack of androgen at this critical point in development causes the brain of the male rat to mature in a feminine way and become responsive to female hormones like the normal female brain does. Thus, in these animals researchers have succeeded in inducing homosexual behaviour notwithstanding normal appearance and normal androgen levels. This cannot be done by any other method. Rats whose testosterone levels are subsequently made normal when they reach maturity are of normal appearance but show strong tendencies to react like females; in the presence of sexually vigorous male rats, most of them respond by arching the hindquarters, which is the normal response of the sexually receptive female. Female-type responses were much more frequent than attempts to mate with receptive females, and some rats have shown feminine sexual behaviour exclusively.

While this role reversal has been shown in research animals, it has yet to be demonstrated in humans. The critical period of sexual differentiation in the human brain probably occurs before birth, in contrast to the rat where it occurs shortly after birth. If so, this opens up the theoretical possibility that hormone disturbances in pregnant women or drugs taken during pregnancy might influence the future sexual orientation of the unborn child, which may have considerable signficance in the aetiology of both homosexuality and transvestism. It is possible that disturbances in the mother provoked by severe stress, if they occur at the critical time, could disturb the endocrine balance of the foetus sufficiently to affect sexual maturation of the brain. An effect of this kind has been produced experimentally by subjecting pregnant female rats to the stress of immobilization under a bright light. When their male offspring grew up, they proved defective in male copulatory performance. This deficiency appeared to be due to some degree of feminization of the brain, since when given female hormones, they presented themselves with arched backs in the manner of a sexually receptive female.

There is one piece of evidence that suggests such behaviour can occur in humans. Male rats whose brains had been feminized by neonatal hormone manipulation showed a characteristic feedback effect in response to oestrogen administration. A similar effect in the shape of a preliminary decrease followed by a steeper increase in the levels of serum progesterone was found to occur in twenty-one homosexual men after an injection of oestrogen but did not occur in twenty heterosexual controls. The difference was not accounted for by lack of androgen in the homosexual group, since their plasma testosterone levels were within the normal range for heterosexual males.

Such research is still in its infancy, and many of the studies remain to be verified by further research. The question of a genetic factor in homosexuality is supported by Kallman's work in 1952, when he reported high concordance rates of homosexuality in identical twins. Subsequent work, however, has cast some doubt on this.

Certainly there is no doubt that psychological influences early in life through child-rearing experiences do have an important effect in the genesis of homosexual orientation. The over-dominating or rejecting parent, repression of early sexual curiosity and discouraging attitudes towards gender-assertive behaviour feature in the backgrounds of many homosexuals. The constellation of close, oppressive mothers and weak, unsympathetic or absent fathers has frequently been identified. Direct learning of homosexual practices during physical sex play between school children does not appear to be relevant unless the youngster has some prior emotional interest in the homosexual relationship or a fear of heterosexuality. West states that when early sex contacts with persons of the same sex take on a romantic flavour and the adolescent falls in love with a member of the same sex, the likelihood of a persisting homosexual orientation is much greater. The importance of pleasurable conditioning experiences favouring the development of sexual behaviour patterns at the time of early orgasmic experience seems to have been over-emphasized by some learning theorists, though its importance cannot be ignored.

Gadpaille summarizes with the following points: (1) Preferential homosexuality is clearly the result of some disorder in the normal programmed sequence of psychosexual differentiation and development. (2) The aetiological effect of early child rearing is reaffirmed as the major influence determining sexual adaptation and maladaptation. (3) The subtlety of foetal hormonal effects and the extreme vulnerability of masculine psychosexual differentiation and maleness in general suggests that one should not expect obvious and dramatic child-parent traumata in case histories of all homosexuals. (4) It is possible that presently undetectable embryonic disorders may produce conditions which make it easier for an individual to develop cross-sex attitudes. (5) The anatomic proximity and functional neural connections between oral and genital excitatory areas may explain the case with which homosexuals are able to substitute oral sexual gratification for heterosexual genital pleasure. (6) Biological research offers support for the analytical theory of bisexuality. (7) The central importance of maternal influence must be reconsidered and greater significance accorded to peer relationships in childhood, particularly childhood sex play.

West (1955) draws attention to animal behaviour and notes

that many species of animals have been seen to behave homosexually. Rasmussen (1955) has demonstrated that male rats given an electric shock whenever they attempted to copulate with females were discouraged from further attempts at heterosexuality but then became homosexual in their drive. Konrad Lorenz (1958) has shown the importance of imprinting. In some species, the imprinting experience determines sexual as well as social responses; at the mating season, faultily imprinted birds perform rituals and copulatory attempts with other species, such as the human objects to which they had become attached as babies. Desmond Morris (1969) notes that creatures arrange themselves in a pecking order. Dominants behave to submissives in a masculine way and treat the submissive ones as female, and the submissives respond in a feminine manner to them. This may have interesting reflections in human society and the advent of the "Woman's Lib" organization. Desmond Morris notes that the cow in heat mounts another cow, demonstrating the presence of sexual drive plus frustration in the absence of the bull.

A review of the aetiology of homosexuality is given in West's book, with some 400 further references relating to the evidence for and against biological and hormonal influences.

Treatment

When we consider treatment for homosexuality, we are back in the dilemma outlined at the beginning of this chapter, namely, whether it is justifiable to view homosexuality as a condition requiring treatment in the first place. Or should we instead be educating society in matters of tolerance so that minority groups, as long as they do nothing to harm others, should be allowed to do their own thing in their own way. This latter role, however, might not be primarily a medical one and should be left to sociological and educational influences.

Perhaps the doctor can best learn to control any prejudices he may have acquired and offer advice to the homosexual who consults him by dealing with the problem objectively, in exactly the same way he would with a heterosexual with a similar problem.

Certain practical problems do arise, however.   An individual may attend at the clinic and voice concern about a suspected homosexual orientation requesting help in dealing with the problems this poses.   These problems may be social, sexual or, depending on where the individual lives, of a legal nature. Erective, orgasmic and ejaculatory problems are virtually non-existent in homosexual groups, which is an interesting point on which to reflect.

The first essential is to establish by careful history taking which of the six categories outlined above seems the most appropriate diagnosis for the individual one is counselling.

For what we have called the *true homosexual* it seems at the present time most appropriate to advise such individuals to come to terms with their situation and accept themselves without feeling inadequacy or shame.   Most states in which homosexuality is not illegal now offer counselling and social agencies run by responsible individuals who are themselves homosexual.   In England the main organization is the Campaign for Homosexual Equality (CHE), and their counselling organization is known as "Friend."   There are branches in most major towns.   Addresses can usually be obtained through Gay News, a British weekly newspaper devoted to homosexual interests.

Any attempt to treat such true homosexuals by altering their sexual orientation towards heterosexuality would seem not to be ethically defensible at the level of our present knowledge nor effective in any case.   Aversion therapy and similar behaviourally orientated therapies have not been shown in general to be effective in this group.

For those groups in whom a bisexual orientation appears, counselling should be directed towards reassurance.   If the individual feels threatened by homosexual contacts in those areas where there are legal problems, straightforward advice on the ways in which such situations can be avoided and a more positive orientation towards heterosexuality is perhaps appropriate.   Usually such individuals who attend the clinics are young and immature and inexperienced.   Their best help lies through channelling their drives.

The treatment of deviancy will be considered in a later chapter. While chemical methods using drugs may sometimes be appropriate in these other groups showing homosexual behaviour, there is no evidence to suggest that drug therapy using hormones or suppressants of sexual drive is of any relevance nor has any influence on true homosexual behaviour in terms of altering the orientation.

Until fairly recently, women's organizations comparable with those that promote the interests of male homosexuals hardly existed. This state of affairs has changed with the upsurge of women's liberation and gay liberation groups both in Europe and America. Magazines are now published for lesbians, and social and counselling services similar to those available for men have been formed. In Britain, the chief lesbian organization is Kenric, which produces a monthly newsletter; monthly magazines *Sappho* and *Arena 3* are also available. The Albany Trust concerns itself with sexual troubles in both sexes and publishes *Man and Society*.

Chapter 12

TRANSVESTISM AND TRANSSEXUALISM

O NE OF THE MAIN problems for the clinician studying aberrant
patterns of behaviour is that he sees the pathological, that is
to say, those cases who are referred because they are ill or cases
that the courts have seen because they have fallen foul of some
particular law.   Some analytical writers seem to have fallen into
the same trap in that they have attempted to extrapolate material
significant within a severely disturbed group and apply it as a
general principle to the rest of the population.

In the same way, much material that is presented to the doctor concerning sexual or gender function is pathological; to de-
duce from this material the behaviour patterns of the general
population exhibiting this trend is to create a further distortion.
This has been particularly true in medical writings on homosexual behaviour in the past and is perhaps even more in evidence when consideration turns to gender identity problems
and in particular that of cross-dressing.

The picture of transvestism presented to the medical student
is one culled from forensic cases of fetishistic masochists who have
accidentally strangled themselves, those convicted of stealing
underwear from clothes-lines and individuals apprehended for
causing a breach of the peace when appearing in public in a
cross-dressed state.

The laws concerning cross-dressing vary widely from country
to country.   In some parts of the world it is irrelevant, and in
some parts of the world, completely tolerated.   In others there
are strict prohibitions against people "masquerading" as the opposite sex.   In many western societies, such behaviour is fully

118

tolerated amongst females but not amongst males, which throws an interesting light on the social attitudes and public mores that movements such as "women's lib" have been challenging.

Individuals may cross-dress for a variety of reasons. Curiously, drag artists are popular in clubs, particularly amongst the female audience in clubs, and in pantomime and other theatrical displays cross-dressing is acceptable and usually seen as humorous. In real life, it tends to be erroneously equated with homosexuality, which is somewhat illogical, when the matter is considered more closely.

Indeed, it is doubtful whether cross-dressing should be considered as coming under the general heading of sexual problems at all, since sexuality is not in itself relevant to the phenomenon. In the cases normally considered under transvestism and transsexualism, it is a distortion of gender identity that provides the key rather than a distortion of sexual performance.

The commonest reason in our society for cross-dressing is that of fashion. In western society, this is almost completely confined to females, and since there are virtually no legal proscriptions against transvestism or indeed against homosexuality amongst females, the most common reaction to a woman who walks through the streets in male attire is a raised eyebrow or two. This is not the situation the other way round, where the male who wears what is commonly accepted as female attire, in this particular context the skirt or dress, is liable to attract considerably more censure and possibly fall foul of the laws against soliciting, importuning or breach of the peace, even though such matters are far from the individual's mind.

In practice, there seems no logic in condemning individuals for what they wear; indeed, in the majority of states in the United States and Great Britain, there is technically no law to prevent this. Public attitudes, however, particularly attitudes of the police, are somewhat different, and suspicion is likely to be aroused if such an individual enters the inappropriate toilet, for example.

Causes of cross-dressing may therefore be listed as follows:
   1. Fashion

2. Entertainment
3. Transvestism
4. Homosexuality
5. Fetishism
6. Transsexualism

The active desire to wear the clothes of the opposite sex in order to identify with some aspect of the other sex is qualitatively different from the wearing of such garments purely for fashion. When a woman wears a trouser-suit, she is not in most cases deriving satisfaction by identifying with a masculine role. She does not wish people to believe that she is a man nor wish to act in a masculine way. Nor is it likely that she wears masculine underwear underneath the suit. This purely follows the dictates of fashion, though why the cross-dressing fashion has developed is a more intriguing question.

If the wearer of garments normally used by the opposite sex derives some positive satisfaction out of this activity, fulfilling some inner need, then the motive is somewhat different.

The desire to wear the clothes of the opposite sex as expressed by transevstites is a desire to express what such an individual sees as aspects within him of the opposite sex. Thus, in the male it is the desire to identify with or to express femininity by adopting the feminine role as that individual sees it. The need to dress may assume an obsessional quality, and the opportunity to do so provides need satisfaction. This bears no relationship to sexual identification, which in the majority of transvestites is heterosexual. Such individuals are introjecting what they see as desirable attributes portrayed in the other sex and wish to incorporate this into their own persons. Let us consider the four relevant sub-groups in our classification in turn.

Transvestism

The incidence of transvestism amongst males has been variously estimated as between 1 in 100 and 1 in 1,000 of the population. The incidence in females has not been accurately measured, since because of the social structure of society, it is unnecessary for the female to identify herself as an out-of-line group. Thus, she sees no need to seek advice or treatment for what appears as a normal enough pattern of behaviour.

The aetiology of transvestism is unclear. Anecdotal evidence has been provided to show distortions in parental relationships or conditioning at an early age through emphasis being paid by the parents to the virtues of the other sex during the individual's childhood. Research by the author outlined in brief later in this chapter has failed to substantiate these as being common elements in the past histories of such individuals. While early conditioning may play a part, it seems more probable that the condition manifests itself through some inborn or parental effect along the lines suggested by West quoted in the chapter on homosexuality (West, 1976).

The sexual orientation of the bulk of transvestites is heterosexual. The pattern the condition takes is characteristic.

The majority of such individuals can identify an interest in the clothing and mannerisms of the opposite sex from an early age, usually around six or seven, and well before puberty. Most research has been done on males; it is easier therefore to present the features from this viewpoint. The boy, if he gets the opportunity, may try on clothes belonging to his sisters or mother, usually in secret and with some feelings of guilt attached. He may get involved in dressing-up games and, unlike the majority of boys, gets some satisfaction at an emotional level from attempts by older sisters to dress him up as a girl perhaps as part of a game. Thus, he is a relatively willing victim of such games and recalls them many years later as having more significance than the average individual might attach to them.

Such phases of interest wax and wane and may not reappear until around puberty when, with increasing sexual awareness, such dressing-up exploits may be associated with masturbatory fantasies but also with a desire to express femininity as the adolescent sees it.

Such boys have no physical characteristics with which to pick them out but are often more interested in what are commonly seen as female pursuits and less inclined to go in for games such as rugger or boxing. They may tend to seek out girls as their friends, envy the opportunity which the girl has to dress up and look pretty, and experiment with make-up and jewelry.

During adolescence, they are likely to go through phases where they acquire clothing of the opposite sex through purchasing a small selection of undergarments or borrowing those belonging to relatives and dressing in them when the opportunity presents itself. Most transvestites describe this feeling as one producing an inner satisfaction, not a sexual thing. Rather they see themselves as being able for a time to dress and behave in a way which to them seems natural and relaxing. It has a tension-relieving effect.

Most such individuals, however, are aware that their peer group would see this behaviour as peculiar and may develop some shame at indulging in it. From time to time, therefore, they may try to "kick the habit" and dispose of any garments they have collected. The behaviour has the elements of an obsessional compulsive state in many ways. Usually the individual, after a period of abstinence of some months or years, feels the need to dress again and begins to acquire a new collection.

The degree to which various individuals take their cross-dressing at this stage is variable. Some may be satisfied with the wearing of underwear, but others want to experiment in the full role and acquire a complete wardrobe, make-up and wig, if necessary, and spend much of their leisure time as females. They may acquire a more extensive knowledge of female interests through magazines and through learning to sew, etc.

At the same time, they are likely to have developed a sexual interest in girls and to have acquired girlfriends. A dilemma exists, therefore, on whether to inform their girlfriend of this interest or to attempt to keep it a secret. Unfortunately for the transvestite, the bulk of women are unlikely to find enjoyment in seeing their male partner adopting a feminine role and prefer a masculine man who will play a more dominant part in their relationship. The transvestite may well fear, therefore, that in revealing this side of his personality he risks losing his partner.

Equally, many transvestites anticipate that once they develop a serious relationship with the opposite sex or marry, their interest in cross-dressing will wane. Unfortunately, this is rarely the case, and after a while the added temptation of the presence of female garments and accessories about the house is likely to tempt them further. At this stage, if they have not told their partners, then there comes an increasing risk of discovery, which can have a considerable psychological impact on the female partner discovering the mate by accident dressed in female clothing. It is often this situation that brings the transvestite to seek help.

A proportion of transvestites may remain in a *forme fruste* of the condition where cross-dressing is used simply in a fetishistic manner. Equally, there are those who wish to adopt a permanent female role and indeed see themselves as female in all but bodily configuration.

Some argument has raged as to whether there is a true distinction between transsexualism, where the individual sees himself or herself as locked in the wrong-shaped body by some unfortunate quirk of fate and who is desirous of a sex change operation in order to put it right, and the full-time transvestite. Some authorities suggest there is a clear-cut distinction between the two, whereas others tend to see it as a continuum, with transsexualism as simply the one extreme.

It seems that circumstances determine to a large degree the extent to which the transvestite feels able to adopt the female role. A large proportion in the author's survey, however, wish they had been born the other sex and would jump at the chance of a magic button being pressed if other factors in their life would allow it.

To many others, however, the cross-dressing seems more a fantasy game that they feel the urge to play from time to time but which does not have an over-powering intensity. These individuals do not wish to relinquish their male genitalia nor their sexual desire for females and prefer a situation where they could be accepted as transvestites by their female acquaintances but still be able to relate sexually to women.

There are complex inter-relationships between gender identity, sexual need and other aspects of personality, so it does not seem possible to generalize too thoroughly. The tendency at present in western society is to minimize the differences between the sexes, and it may well be that transvestism will prove to be an artificial concept. No particular reason exists why one sex should need to follow what society sees as the stereotyped role for them to play, while fashions of dressing have already led to a situation where the female can wear anything she wishes. In the transvestite's ideal society, therefore, those who wish to identify and live in the role of the sex opposite from their genetically determined one would be fully free to do so. Society would accept them as it might accept other minority groups without discrimination. In this sense, therefore, the transvestite does not see himself as sick or as matching in any way the medical model.

In those in whom the condition is fully manifest, the adoption of a full-time feminine role may be possible, particularly if their physique lends itself to passing in society in the female role and being accepted as such. A number of cases are known to the author where this has been successfully accomplished, and some well-known historical figures also fall into this category.

The history of transvestism is interesting. The name is said to have been coined by Hirschfield in 1910. Ellis (1936) described the condition as a state of psychosexual inversion and used the term *eonism* after the character d'Eon, a French diplomat at the court of St. James who lived as a woman for much of his life. Transsexualism was used by Benjamin (1953) to describe the wish to change the anatomical sex.

The practice of cross-dressing is found as a cultural variant in many societies, as referred to by Randall (1959) in a study of fifty cases. Lukianowicz (1959) states that transvestism is known under various names in almost all cultures and in all parts of the world. Its ubiquity led Ellis to the conclusion that it might represent not a corrupt or over-refined manifestation of late cultures, but rather the survival of an ancient and natural tendency of more primitive man.

The phenomenon was already known in antiquity. It was described by Harodotes as the "Skythian illness" on the North shores of the Black Sea. Its existence in classical Greece is shown in a picture of Hercules dressed in female clothes and serving his mistress Omphale. Transvestism was known in ancient Rome where some of the Roman emperors, for example Caligula and Heliogabal, occasionally dressed in female garments.

In more recent times, the brother to King Henri III of France, the Abbé de Choisey and the Chavalier d'Eon were all well-known figures in France.

Masson (1935) surveyed the history, literature and ethnography covering 1838 to 1935 and found descriptions of sixty-nine cases by twenty-nine authors.

Prince (1971), himself an admitted transvestite, has written a complete book describing for the male all that he requires to know for complete satisfactory transvestite conversion.

There is not a great deal in conventional medical literature; recent articles by Stoller (1971) and a brief reference by Bentler and Prince (1970) give a few further references. Lukianowicz (1959) surveyed various aspects of transvestism and concluded that psychologically the transvestite does not differ markedly from the non-transvestite, though as a group in treatment, they may be more introverted, neurotic and obsessional than control groups. Bentler and Prince have shown through a discriminate function analysis comparing the mean scores on nineteen scales for transvestites and controls that the groups can be differentiated at only a marginal level of significance. There were no gross differences detectable between transvestites and controls on neurotic or psychotic scales.

Apart from the Beaumont Society, a literature of magazines such as *Transvestia* and others exists, and advertisements are commonly found in the more avant-garde dating magazines. Descriptive literature has a small readership, since to the non-transvestite it is of limited appeal. There is, however, some interesting descriptive literature; in particular, Raynor (1966) gives an interesting insight into the sub-culture as it exists in the United States.

A characteristic fantasy of many transvestites seems to be

that they should be forced by females to dress in female clothing and then be accepted by them. This gives rise to the transvestite association with bondage and forms of humiliation and punishment of a masochistic kind which may be available through prostitutes who cater to this desire, who may provide domination for those of submissive nature who may take on the role of maids and enjoy a relationship of being mastered by their female partner. This, however, is not characteristic of the group as a whole, but rather of the more deviant sub-culture which is catered to in the larger metropolises.

For the transsexual who wishes for a sex change, Prince considers in detail in his book the problems to be faced by anybody who undertakes this irrevocable step. This subject is also considered by Hoopes et al. (1968) and by Pauly (1965), who discusses the current status of the change of sex operation. Postoperative results of 121 male transsexuals who had obtained sex reassignment surgery were reviewed. Satisfactory outcome was 10 times more likely than unsatisfactory result if careful screening of the patients was made. The majority of patients who request this operation are males wishing to become females. Pauly states: "At the present time one is impressed with the lack of success in attempting to alter gender identity once established, by traditional psychotherapy. This fact together with the apparent success of sex-reassignment surgery compels one to accept the surgical treatment of transsexualism on an experimental basis until the initial results can be verified or contradicted, or until alternative treatment procedures prove successful."

Not all authors, however, are so optimistic. Cases of genital self-mutilation were found in 18 percent of cases reviewed from the literature, though many of these may have been patients suffering from schizophrenia. The patients may be orientated to a love relationship with males. Pauly reviews in further references the writings on transsexualism in the world medical literature. The majority of reports are only on single cases, however, or small numbers. Roth and Ball (1964) reported on a number of cases and made the important distinction between transsexualism and other conditions.

Transsexuals pursue their desire for sex change with a fanaticism matched only, as Hoenig (1970) states, by the equally strange resentment and intolerance of society towards them. This clash very often leads, not only to the alienation of the patient from those around him, but even to a vindictive hostility from those to whom he turns for help. The condition is often noted in retrospect from early puberty and is usually established by the early twenties. Benjamin (1953) found early signs of transsexualism in 84 percent in early childhood, 4 percent in puberty and 12 percent after this time. Hoenig states that these patients show a high incidence of concomitant psychiatric disorders. The home background was abnormal in 30 percent of cases. Educational adjustment did not seem grossly impaired, but work adjustment was often poor. Anti-social behaviour was widespread and occurred in 47 percent of patients; prostitution was common.

A study by the author of 220 transvestites, members of the Beaumont Society, a social and counselling self-help group in Britain for heterosexual cross-dressers, showed the following characteristics.

The mean age of respondents was 44.6 years, S.D. being 11.9 years. The first recalled cross-dressing, which was not associated with orgasmic experience, occurred at mean age 9.9 years, S.D. 6.8 years; that is, 50 percent started well before puberty.

Of the total, 64 percent were married, and 98 percent considered themselves heterosexual, although 30 percent were bisexual when in a transvestite role, at least in fantasy. An ongoing heterosexual relationship was present in 63 percent, but 53 percent were submissive in their heterosexual role. The orgasmic rate was on the low side compared with the heterosexual norm of Kinsey. Thus, 40 percent had orgasm less than once a week, and only 15 percent had a daily average frequency.

Aetiological factors in the early history could not be identified. About 34 percent believed their parents had wished for a girl; in such families, the father was often seen as ineffective and the mother as dominant. There was a .05 level of correlation between this factor and transsexualism. Those who preferred to have been born a woman numbered 65 percent. Some 29 per-

cent had "progressed" to transsexualism; that is, they saw themselves as female and wished for sex change.   While only 2 percent had gender re-orientation surgery, 48 percent lived as much
of their lives as possible in a female role.

As children, 6 percent of respondents had been aware of envy-
ing girls their clothes, and 4 percent observed that they had tried
to escape what they saw as a masculine stereotype to which they
could not aspire.   Approximately 5 percent were aware of a close
relative who cross-dressed.   Even though 10 percent had been
"seduced" into cross-dressing by older siblings or adults, the significant point is that 90 percent had not had these experiences.
Therefore, they are of no relevance in the aetiology of cross-dressing.

The Maudesley personality inventory scores showed a mean
of 21 on the extroversion scale and a 26.6 on the neuroticism
scale.   Of the total number, 37 percent had an extroversion score
of less than 17; that is, they were highly introverted.   Thus, the
respondents were in general more introverted and neurotic in
profile than a control group.

Thus the common fallacies about cross-dressers are by and
large disproved; although introverted, the group was little dissimilar from the rest of the population in all the criteria assessed.

What then should be the therapist's aim if an individual with
transvestite leanings seeks advice in the clinic?   This would depend to some extent on the model which the therapist adopts.
There seems little reason to discourage an individual from wearing whatever clothes he or she finds most comfortable; if men
wish to adopt a feminine role, then as long as no one else is hurt
thereby, there seems little reason to discourage them or to see
them as "sick."   A simple parallel would perhaps be the woman
who wishes to play football or box or learn joinery.   Nevertheless, society is still liable to equate transvestism with homosexuality and to suspect the motives of the cross-dresser.   Men are liable
to feel somewhat threatened by such an individual and the implications of importuning, and the police are liable to be suspicious.
Wives may equally feel threatened by a partner with such interests.   For all these reasons, the transvestite may indeed require

counselling, though if effective treatment existed to remove entirely their interest, most would not wish to do so. They see this as a complimentary part of their personality, not as something perverted that should be extinguished. Rather they wish that society would accept them, and it is perhaps this acceptance by society with which the specialists should concern themselves.

Nevertheless, the transvestite, like the homosexual, may seek guidance. As things stand at present, it does not seem effective to attempt to remove the desire to cross-dress. Behavioural methods such as aversion therapy have had little real success, and the ethical arguments for using such treatment on these individuals are dubious. Should one give electric shocks to a female who wants to do joinery? The parallel is not entirely irrelevant.

The same problem presents itself in childhood as with homosexuality. If a child is recognized as developing transvestite interests, should the parents or teachers encourage or discourage or ignore? Should an attempt be made to channel the child into attitudes more appropriate, to satisfy society's views on the sex roles, knowing that such an individual may bring problems upon himself in later life if he persists in this behaviour pattern? There do not seem at present to be any clear answers to such questions, but the ability to identify such individuals in their early years would make the question of more than academic interest.

Perhaps the most appropriate role the therapist can play is that of counsellor. The transvestite who is developing a relationship with a partner is probably best advised to make the partner aware of this interest. It is then up to the partner to accept or reject before the relationship has become a committed one. In situations where the couple is already married and the secret becomes public knowledge, then counselling of the couple, and in particular the wife, will be necessary. This should be designed to create understanding sympathy and hopefully a new awareness of the partner as an individual. In this way the marriage may be strengthened rather than disrupted.

As with homosexuals, in the author's view such individuals are best put in touch with expert counselling agencies who specialize in this particular problem.   In Great Britain, there exists an organization for heterosexual transvestites known as the Beaumont Society; this agency provides counselling through the Beaumont Trust as well as social activities where individuals can meet others with similar interests and other couples who have faced similar problems in conditions where they feel secure.

An equivalent organization exists in the United States in the shape of S.S.S. or Tri Sigma.   The organizations run magazines or newsletters and provide advice on such matters as make-up and dress, legal problems that may be encountered and some fantasy literature.   Most cities have a branch.

Some individuals who are living full-time in the role may request hormone therapy in order to decrease sexual interest or to induce breast development.   The individual circumstances of such persons must be considered carefully, preferably by a clinic that specializes in psychosexual problems, before such treatment can be advised or recommended.

The Homosexual Transvestite

Just as transvestism seems to be reasonably common in society, so is homosexuality which, according to Kinsey, may exist in some 10 percent of the population.

Thus, one would anticipate that if 1 in 10 males is homosexual and 1 in 100, for the sake of argument, is a transvestite, 1 in 1,000 would be both transvestite and homosexual purely by chance.   Thus, in a city of half a million inhabitants, one might anticipate around 500 such individuals.   This is a significant number, though considerably smaller than one would anticipate for the heterosexual transvestite or the non-transvestite homosexual.   In addition to this group, however, one must recognize that there are a number of transvestites who, although heterosexual in their orientation when in the male role, do nevertheless fantasize when in the female role that they might have a sexual relationship with a man who treats them and accepts them as female.   Some indeed may have the opportunity to act out this fantasy but would not consider themselves homosexual in this situation, but rather as acting in their true gender role.

In general, normal homosexuals do not cross-dress. This should come as no surprise since if a male is basically attracted to other males, he is hardly likely to want them to masquerade in the role of a female, a sex with whom he does not wish to relate sexually. Thus, the non-transvestite homosexual tends to avoid the company of those known as "drag queens" and does not find such individuals sexually attractive. Some bisexual individuals, however, may be attracted by the novelty of such situations, and some homosexual transvestites, if promiscuous by nature, can find ready-made partners and even earn a living by prostitution as is seen in the Catemites of Boogie Street in South-East Asia (Egerton, 1973).

A larger number of male transvestites may engage occasionally in mutual masturbatory activity. It is doubtful whether this implies true homosexuality, but rather it is an extension of narcissistic attitudes in individuals who by force of circumstance are denied a fuller heterosexual activity. The male transvestite who wants a male partner who will treat him as a female may find he has a rather limited choice. Equally, the full-time transvestite who wishes heterosexual partners may only be able to find women who are dominant by nature and have sado-masochistic impulses. Some transvestites exhibit masochistic sexual leanings, but by and large heterosexual transvestites are more introverted individuals than the general population, and their sexual drive as evidenced by the average orgasmic rate is lower than the general population.

This does not seem so true of the homosexual transvestite, who in general adopts a passive role in the sexual experience, allowing the male partner to indulge in anal intercourse with him, but less research has been done on this group.

If such individuals attend the clinic for advice, then it seems most appropriate to deal with the individual problems present rather than to attempt undesired changes in either sexual or gender orientation. As people, they have the same problems as other people; there is no more reason to treat them differently than to differentiate a redhead with a bunion from a brunette with the same disorder.

The Fetishistic Transvestite

The problem of fetishism will be dealt with in the chapter on deviancy. Fetishism implies sexual arousal in response to or in association with the specific objects. These are often inanimate and may be rubberwear, leatherwear or particular types of sexual fantasy situations, for example taking a masochistic role such as playing the role of maid or schoolgirl and dressing accordingly. The motivation of some transvestites appears to have a largely fetishistic component, but these are in the minority compared with the other groups we have considered. Such individuals do not wish to masquerade as women or to socialize as normal females and adopt feminine role playing. Rather they fixate on particular types of clothing where the texture of the garment, for example soft silks or satins, or particular types of garments such as tight-lacing corsets, may be the trigger enabling them to achieve sexual arousal, and without such sexual activity is unsatisfactory. Such individuals may have a compulsion to collect certain types of garments such as nylon panties; it is in these cases that courts occasionally find before them a person who has acquired by stealing from clothes-lines a large collection of underwear, which are stored or used for masturbatory activity if at all.

Again, since deviant behaviour is not uncommon, it is likely that a percentage of transvestites will be deviant and a percentage of those who enjoy deviant sexual behaviour pursuits will be transvestite. As with homosexuality, this may be a purely coincidental overlap in the same sense as some schizophrenics might develop appendicitis and some people with appendicitis might become schizophrenic. There is, however, no condition of schizo-appendicitis which requires separate delineation as a syndrome in its own right.

Such deviant activity can be treated by behavioural methods, and in particular by aversion therapy if it seems justified, though such behaviour seems harmless enough as long as it does not break the law nor offend others and is hardly a matter for medical intervention.

Transsexualism

As has been stated earlier, the borderline between transvestism and transsexualism is a fine one, the bulk of transsexuals having gone through a transvestite phase. Many more transvestites would probably wish for sex change if all they needed to do was take a tablet. Perhaps the key to the difference lies in the mental attitude, for whereas transvestites who are not wholly committed may see transvestism as a way to express femininity but nevertheless retain male genitalia, transsexuals are happy to jettison the outer trappings of what they see to be the wrong sex, since they do not value the ability to express themselves sexually in the gender in which they unwittingly have found themselves. Thus, sexual appetites are usually low, and sexual orientation often tends towards those the transsexual sees as heterosexual mates, even though physically they are the same sex as themselves.

This conviction of being trapped in the wrong body manifests itself at an early age, though unsophisticated adolescents may not be able to formulate this concept fully for themselves at the beginning. The thrill of dressing in clothes of the opposite sex seems less of a driving force, since they consider it natural enough to wear them; clothes are not the important thing.

Occasionally, a patient with psychotic illness is seen whose conviction of sex change is a manifestation of a delusional system. In the author's experience, however, this is a rare phenomenon, whereas transsexualism as we have defined it is probably present in something like 1 in 5,000 of the population. In no way can this group be identified as psychotic or suffering from any type of mental illness, contrary to the writings of some other workers.

While the incidence of requests for sex change operations has been higher in men, perhaps in part due to the more practical aspects of the operation itself, transsexualism seems more common in women vis-à-vis men than is transvestism itself, though not as common.

The problem of how to advise such individuals presenting at

a clinic is one about which there is considerable controversy. The relative success of some so-called sex change operations and their portrayal in the popular press has led to an increase in the number of requests from people who previously had thought that such a thing was an impossible dream for them. Decisions, however, on how to carry out such operative interference should be most carefully considered before any steps are taken, since the result is irreversible.

Nevertheless, the transsexual wishes to function as a member of the opposite sex in practical and sometimes sexual ways. It should be emphasized that transsexuals as we have defined them are physically normal. There is no hermaphroditism, no detectable genetic abnormality and no chromosomal abnormality. The gonads also are normal. Unless and until such time as more subtle hormonal or prenatal influences can be identified, a sex change operation starts with a person who is physically normal, rather than pathologically diseased, and submits them to mutilating surgery, creating what is in effect a neuter state, since there is no way that the gonads of the opposite sex can be grafted or that such an individual can truly take on the attributes of the desired sex. At best, the individuals will mimic the form of the other sex; although they may be able to function in one sense sexually, the transformation is in no way complete.

Some psychiatrists consider that to recommend such treatment at all is to encourage a fantasy world which can never be in the individual's best interest. If we are to take this line, however, we must consider what alternative help can be offered to such people, who may well be subjected to what they see as an intolerable situation for the rest of their lives. Suicide is not unknown.

Firstly, the psychiatrist can give supportive counselling to such individuals advising them to accept the status quo and to live their lives as a full-time transvestite, perhaps with suitably altered work permits and certificates to allow them to live as their chosen sex. With the aid of some hormone therapy and depilation for the man, this might be acceptable. But for many it does not satisfy their craving to be fully accepted among the sex to which they wish to belong. There is always the chance of exposure. There may be difficulties in all sorts of minor ways, for instance the assignment of the correct ward if they need admission to hospital or medicals at work. Some legal risks might apply, for example, should there be a complaint made against them of masquerading. Neither can they function genitally in their desired sex with regard to urination or any sexual contact with others. Nevertheless, for those whose physique is quite obviously such that they will never be able to pass satisfactorily as the other sex or whose personalities seem to show some level of instability that would make the chances of operative intervention less successful, counselling can ethically be the only sensible course to adopt.

The second line of management lies in treating the condition of transsexualism in the sense of altering the patient's mental set in order to remove the desire for sex change and to allow such individuals to function heterosexually and normally within the sex to which they have been born. Unfortunately, gender orientation in adults appears singularly unmodifiable by present methods of treatment. While some success has been claimed with behavioural methods in adolescents who have developed such gender distortions, the success of aversion therapy or any other kind of behavioural manipulation in adults has been singularly lacking. Psychotherapy and drug treatment are equally ineffective. Thus, at present, this option is of somewhat academic interest and is unlikely to receive much co-operation from an individual whose main desire is quite the reverse.

The third option, therefore, open to the therapist in those cases where there is a stable personality and a long-standing conviction of the desire for sex change and where no interest or satisfaction is obtained from heterosexual genital activity is to pursue the prospect of sex reassignment.

Most clinics who counsel such individuals agree that it is necessary to ensure that the individual has been able to function in the sex role which they wish to adopt for at least two years pre-operatively. During this period of time, the snags as well as the virtues of the change will have been brought home to many.

It will have been possible for them to receive hormone treatment and to begin to make some of the necessary adjustments in terms of obtaining proper documentation through the appropriate authorities and to learn the mannerisms and attitudes of their new sex in order that they may pass comfortably when the time comes. In the male, depilation of facial hair can be carried out, which is often quite a long process extending over eighteen months or more. Many transsexuals have a rather idealized view of how the other sex functions, and it may well be that the job they will be able to obtain after sex reassignment will pay less than that held before. The consequences and the limitations of the operation must also be fully discussed.

In other words, there is considerable preparatory work to be done before such an operation is performed, and indeed, considerable work needs to be done after the operation to help such people through the required social adjustments. To neglect this side of the problem is most unwise and indeed ethically indefencible since so much of the success of the operation depends on these factors.

Considerable expertise has been developed in certain centres by plastic surgeons who have agreed to undertake sex reassignment surgery. Nevertheless, such operations must be carried out in a number of stages. They are painful. Complications such as graft rejection or infection can also be a big problem, and by no means therefore are all operations 100 percent successful. Many patients are disappointed with the final result, although the majority seem to feel that even a relatively poor result is better than their original state.

For a detailed description of the techniques, the reader must look to more specialized publications. In brief, however, the procedure in the male is to cause breast development and softening of the hair and voice by the use of oestrogen preparations. The first stage of the operation is then to remove the penis and testicles, if possible keeping some tissue intact in order to subsequently graft an artificial passageway to function as a vagina. The urethral meatus is fashioned to open at the skin surface, but in the process, some of the muscles which assist in controlling urine flow are inevitably lost. Subsequently, plastic tidying-up operations may be necessary to make the artificial vagina more effective. Regular dilatation with dilators is required to prevent the orifice from closing off. Minor degrees of plastic surgery may be helpful to the face or chest, but breast implants are not usually necessary.

Simple castration and penectomy are straightforward enough procedures but are not usually sufficient to satisfy the patient. The success in creating artificial vaginas that are functional without being painful on intercourse with a male is a more difficult task and is not always successful. However, at this stage the patient is at least superficially functionally female and can exist in a female world without fear of exposure or ridicule. The ability to ejaculate is lost, of course, as is the ability to experience climax through the penis. Some post-operative transsexuals claim that they are still capable of orgasmic release; whether this is entirely a psychological affair or whether the retention of some of the nerves supplying the genitalia through careful surgery allows orgasm to be triggered is not entirely clear. Orgasm is a subtle procedure that can be triggered in states of high excitement by stimulation completely divorced from the genitalia, so it may well be that this is possible. However, the loss of orgasmic ability does not seem to matter very much to most, as it was a rare enough event in the pre-operative state.

The author has noted with interest how some transsexuals who were at pains to emphasize their femininity in manner and in dress before the operation become less attractive as women and less interested in their appearance when they feel their goal has been achieved and they can relax and be their natural selves.

In the female-to-male operative procedure, testosterone may be given in order to induce male-type hair growth and clitoral enlargement. The breasts are usually amputated and the ovaries and uterus removed in one procedure. The outer labial folds can be freed and joined together to fashion a scrotum into which artificial testes can be placed. The enlarged clitoris can be freed from the underlying tissue, and it may be possible to fashion a passageway to allow the urethra to traverse the clitoris and urine to be passed in the normal male manner, though this has been a singularly unsuccessful technique to date. The finished result, if successful, may then appear as a rather small and immature penis that is capable of some erectile response, as is the clitoris, but is not able to function fully as a penetrative organ such as would satisfy a heterosexual female nor, of course, is it capable of ejaculation, though the ability to climax will be retained.

It will be appreciated that the complications of such procedures in both sexes can be considerable. The administration of hormones appropriate to the other sex is not without hazard in terms of inducing hypertrophy of tissue and conceivably subsequent carcinomatous change. The use of testosterone in the female before breast amputation may produce mastitic change, and similarly, enlargement of the male breast by oestrogens can cause problems which need long-term post-operative follow-up.

Despite the snags, however, the author has seen many individuals living considerably more contented lives and functioning in society effectively in their new role following such operations. It does not seem reasonable, therefore, to take the line adopted by some colleagues that this procedure should never in any circumstances be embarked upon. Given careful pre-operative assessment and proper follow-up, the patient may be able to live a contented life, something which was quite impossible for them before and which is unlikely to be achieved by the other available treatment options.

Chapter 13

SEXUAL DEVIANCY

A PROBLEM THAT RUNS throughout the subject of sexual perversion is that of where the line of normal behaviour begins and ends. Patterns of sexual response have varied widely within different historical times, within different cultures and even within sub-groups in particular communities. Our discussion on sexual norms and the work of Kinsey have shown that it is impossible to lay down rules of normality; indeed, there seems little purpose in making this artificial attempt. Nevertheless, most countries' ecclesiastical and civil laws have put certain types of sexual activity beyond the bounds of legality, and penalties have been and sometimes still are severe. The logic of this is hard to determine, seeming to relate to the prejudices of the communities' lawmakers at any given time.

Thus, if one attempts to define sexual normality as behaviour that is geared towards heterosexual mating or is a preliminary to this, we immediately exclude the most common and so statistically the most normal sexual activity, namely masturbation. Indeed, at some stages in adolescent development it is probable that homosexual activity is slightly more frequent than heterosexual; again, statistically this would be the norm.

Perhaps the most satisfactory definition of sexual deviancy or perversion might be that when patterns of behaviour not normally directed towards heterosexual mating become dominant in an individual's life to the extent that without this behaviour the individual is rendered sexually ineffective, i.e. impotent or frigid, and such behaviour becomes an end in itself rather than a prelude to copulation, then such behaviour can reasonably be described as deviant. By this definition, of course, we would be bound to include homosexuality, so perhaps the definition could be extended to include both heterosexual and homosexual mating as the prerequisite of normality.

Is there any thread that runs through deviancy problems and ties them together? Recalling the initial remarks on classification, it will be remembered that one factor commonly found was a degree of inadequacy or immaturity of sexual functioning. Many such individuals were not fully potent or orgasmic except under special conditions in which the depth of emotional intimacy in the relationship was diminished to some degree.

Another factor that requires consideration is the curious problem as to why deviant sexual behaviour is apparently so much more common in males. The type of deviancy found in individuals appears to be fluid. That is to say that while imprinting or the development of conditioned responses to certain stimuli may cause individuals to favour some particular type of deviant activity, nevertheless, many individuals adopt a variety of different behaviour patterns in which the need for novelty appears to be the determining factor. One should perhaps not accept the statement that deviancy is more common in males until one has looked a little bit more carefully at the social implications of deviant behaviour and the definition of what may be included under the general heading of deviancy in the first place.

Legal prohibitions against deviant behaviour have been designed to protect to some extent the innocent or weak individual from seduction or exploitation by another. This has inclined the law to see more of a threat in male behaviour patterns that deviate from the norm than similar patterns in females. Thus, the fear of rape is principally a female phenomenon partly because of the structure of society and partly because for intercourse to take place between male and female, the male of necessity must be sexually aroused in order for erection to be present, whereas in the female this need not be the case. Similarly, male homosexual behaviour has led to the passing of laws in many states which were originally associated more with prohibitions against anal intercourse than with a relationship between two people of the same sex.

Furthermore, society's tolerance of such practices as indecent exposure again reflect this threat aspect. If a male feels the urge to expose himself to a female, this may be seen by the female as a threat, where the expectation, though usually erroneous, is of sexual assault. If a female exposes to the male, it is likely to be seen not as a threat but as an invitation which the male can accept or reject depending on circumstances. It is not, however, seen as a threat, and thus society sees no need to litigate against it.

In practice, offences of indecent exposure are much more frequently found in males than in females if one looks at court cases. It must be remembered, however, that the female who has a desire to expose herself can in most western societies not only do so with impunity but can do so in front of a large audience on the stage and get paid in the process. Equality of the sexes has not yet allowed the male anything like this degree of licence.

Another factor which may explain this sex difference is the innate difference in sexual responsiveness between male and female. Whether this is an inborn or acquired factor, it is nevertheless true that males tend to be more aroused by visual stimuli. This applies to the coquettish or provocative behaviour of the female as well as to pornographic literature where displays of the female form and sexual acts have an erotic effect on the male viewer. Females tend to be more aroused by tactile stimuli, that is to say by what the male does to the female who has acted provocatively towards him, and less to the female equivalent of the girlie magazine. Thus, there is more demand for female strippers than male strippers, and most males want to possess a pornograph! These factors no doubt explain the sex difference in crimes of voyeurism.

Pornographic material, however, is seen by society as portraying sexual activity in visual form, commonly deviant in nature. The female equivalent of this is perhaps the short and over-sentimentalized romantic story so common in women's magazines, where what is portrayed is an account of what the male does to the females in terms of wooing. This has similar erotic connotations for the female that the girlie magazine has for the male and could reasonably be considered just as pornographic, though society for some reason is likely to see it as less depraved.

Should prostitution be included as a type of deviant behaviour? Certainly it can be argued that by our definition, the sexual activity is frequently normal and heterosexual, apart from the financial aspects of the contract. On the other hand, much sado-masochistic activity occurs between prostitutes and clients, and apart from the financial inducements in our society which make prostitution a more attractive proposition to the female, there is evidence from a variety of sources that females with personality problems and from broken home backgrounds often take up prostitution. It is this same group among males who tends to develop other patterns of deviant behaviour.

We are perhaps not really seeing less deviancy in the female than in the male, but rather we are looking at aspects of deviancy which are male-orientated because of the legal circumstances and which reflect society's fears or preoccupations rather than the nature of sexual activity between couples.

Fetishistic behaviour may seem at first to be an exception to this proposition since males much more frequently seem to need particular conditions operating in order to obtain erection than do females to obtain equivalent arousal. On the other hand, many females are not arousable by conventional heterosexual intercourse and need special conditions such as particular types of alternative stimulation or particular types of romantic build-up if they are to achieve climax. Here we may be seeing exactly the same process, allowance having been made for the differing needs of the two sexes, as outlined above.

Incidence of Deviation

In the total population, some 8 percent of males had had sexual experience with animals. This rises to 17 percent among boys raised on farms. Commonly, this behaviour occurs in adolescents exposed to the situation, and often in those of lower I.Q. (Kinsey, 1948). It may also be found in another situation more typical of deviancy, which is a service offered by prostitutes as an abnormal variant of their normal trade.

In the female, the cumulative incidence of homosexual response was 28 percent, and in fact, homosexual response to orgasm occurs about half as frequently in females as in males. The larger proportion of females with homosexual contacts have restricted their activities to a single partner. With regard to animal contacts, 3.6 percent of females were found to have had erotic contact, but only 0.4 percent to orgasm. These were either of an exploratory nature in adolescence, usually with family pets, or as prostitutes in the course of their trade.

Fetishism is described by Kinsey as being an almost exclusively male phenomenon, having seen only two or three cases in their data of females regularly aroused by objects not directly connected with sexual activity. They suggest that this is due to the fact the male is more easily conditioned by his sexual experience and by objects that are associated with these experiences than is the female. Transvestism is stated as being fifty times as common in the male than in the female, but the figures are not given. Hamilton (1939) found 69 percent in his study admitted to some experience of voyeurism. The condition is rarer among females.

Aetiology

Theories on the aetiology of deviance fall naturally into three groups. There are those who believe that genetic and/or biochemical or hormonal disturbances play a leading part in the inability of the individual to conform to normal sexual functioning. Secondly, there are those who consider that early environment plays an important role; they explain the development of deviance on the basis of analytical concepts. And finally, there are those who, while considering early environment to be the key to the problem, apply learning theory and behaviouristic concepts, believing that deviant behaviour is a maladaptive piece of imprinting. It is probable from research into these problems that all three play a part in some or most individuals, since emotional immaturity, the presence of trigger experiences producing erotic imprinting and measurable differences in hormonal and physical factors have been shown in different individuals studied.

Storr (1964), in the introduction to his review of sexual deviation, outlines the general concepts stated above: "The use of
the term deviation implies the existence of a standard of normality from which deviation may take place, but no such absolute
standard can be found, for what is considered to be sexually normal varies widely both from country to country and from epoch
to epoch. A sexual practice which is considered acceptable in
one time and place may be abhorred as a perversion in another
and even within the same culture each individual may adhere to
a different standard of sexual behaviour depending upon the interaction between his upbringing and the strength of his sexual
needs. It is safe to assert that there is no sexual practice which
has not somewhere been condemned and none which has not
elsewhere been accepted."

It seems clear from the work of ethologists that in most species, critical stages are reached in development where imprinting
of a sexual nature may take place. Should early sexual experiences be intense but the arousal take place in an abnormal situation, this pattern of behaviour may be continued throughout the
animal's life despite later opportunities for normal heterosexual
experience. While this has not been established as relevant to
human sexual behaviour, it seems reasonable that the possibility
may well exist. An additional factor in human beings, however,
is the development of sexual guilt, which is commonly found in
the upbringing of children in western society. The taboo on
incest is sanctified by a long history and is noted in Freud's theories of sexuality. Even here, however, it should be noted that
certain societies have accepted incest as normal within some
groups, such as the preservation of a royal line.

Sexual inferiority is another important point. Confidence
that one is or can be lovable is an important factor in the secur-
ity of the individual. Promiscuity is not generally considered
to be a sexual deviation, but it is a failure to achieve a mature
sexual relationship. An opinion of sexual inferiority is commonly found in people suffering from sexual deviation, and such
a conviction has two roots. The first is a generalized feeling of

being unlovable, which may often be attributed to an early failure in the relationship between child and mother. The second is a more specific inability of the male or female to identify with the current role assigned by society.

Certain differences between males and females in the relative frequencies of types of deviation emphasize the importance of the different roles given to male and female within society. This is emphasized by Margaret Mead (1962); "The recurrent problem of civilization is to define the male role satisfactorily enough, whether it be to build gardens or to raise cattle, kill game or kill enemies, build bridges or handle bank shares, so that the male may in the course of his life reach a solid sense of irreversible achievement of which his childhood knowledge of the satisfactions of childbearing have given him a glimpse."

In many cases of sexual deviation, it can be shown that a parent of the same sex has failed the child by being a deficient sexual model. A mother who has never herself accepted her feminine role may under-value femininity; a father who is less than normally assertive may inhibit his son's masculine development by failing to indicate that there are times when he should stand up for himself.

Greenacres (1968), in a discussion of Robert Bak's paper "The Phallic Woman. The Ubiquitous Fantasy in Perversions," discusses the genetic and dynamic background of the development of these conditions and presents the analytical point of view with particular reference to the incidence of fetishism. She states that in the development of perversions, due to early disturbances in the mother-infant relationship there is a severe impairment of object relationships that combines with a specifically determined weakness of the body-image and self-image, especially involving the genitalia. This becomes most significant during the phallic and oedipal periods when castration anxiety is extraordinarily acute due to the quality of the aggression aroused at those times.

Patterns of Deviancy

Notwithstanding what has been said in the introduction, there emerge certain patterns of deviant behaviour which are relevant in terms of medical practice and therefore within the remit of this book.   These fall into four major groups, other bizarre minority variants of sexual behaviour being more of forensic interest or merely descriptive terms for items of novel behaviour devised by those whose deviant behaviour nevertheless falls into one of the four groups to be described.

The four categories are as follows: (1) paedophilia, (2) exhibitionism and voyeurism, (3) fetishism, and (4) sado-masochism. Each of these will be considered in turn.

Paedophilia

In paedophilia, sexual arousal and gratification are obtained through relationships with children.   In most western states, any overt sexual activity with a child is illegal, although the age at which childhood is deemed to end and the penalties of such behaviour vary considerably from country to country and from state to state.   Penalties also vary whether the child is male or female, curiously enough, the penalties in many states being more severe for sexual interference with a male child than for sexual interference with a female, which is considered more "normal" even though one would think the damage in terms of potential pregnancy in the older child would certainly be a matter of concern.

Considerable misconceptions, however, arise in the mind of the general public with regard to the definition of childhood. Paedophile organizations which attempt to change the law so that sexual activity with some categories of minors might be legalized are commonly condemned by public opprobrium through the mass media on the unfounded assumption that such individuals wish to legalize sex between mature adults and young children, i.e. those under thirteen.   This is not the case as a rule. However, in the East, child prostitution is not uncommon, as indeed was the case in Britain a century ago.   Indeed, in 1885, the journalist W.T. Stead was able to buy a girl of thirteen for £10 and keep her in a brothel.

Not uncommonly, the child is a willing partner to these endeavours and may indeed encourage them, sometimes for the financial gain which may accrue. Equally, when an offence of this kind is committed by an elderly person, it may well be the presenting symptom of an underlying dementia.

The man who suffers from paedophilia as a true deviation does not do so from excess of sensuality, but rather because he has been unable to find sexual satisfaction in an adult relationship. It is his timid inability to make contact with contemporaries that drives him to focus sexual interest where he can be the undoubted dominant partner. It is relatively rare to find the condition in females, at any event in the courts, though seduction of children by nannies and similar persons with access to children is not uncommon. Kinsey states: "Some of the more experienced students of juvenile problems have come to believe that the emotional reactions of the parents, police officers and other adults who discover that a child has had such contact may disturb the child more seriously than the sexual contacts themselves."

Nowadays, the courts usually recognize that adults who make assaults on children require medical and psychiatric treatment rather than punishment and usually are referred for this to be effected. The disabled may be particularly liable to find themselves in such situations.

It is worth noting, as does West in his book on homosexuality, that sexual fondling of children is not uncommon in some communities and may be encouraged in puberty as a method of teaching children the proper adult ways to behave with their peer group. The strong taboos of western society against children coming into contact with adult sexuality ensures that however much they enjoy sex games among themselves, they take fright if approached by an adult, even though the typical paedophile as a rule is a timorous, inhibited male who solicits with pathetic gentleness.

Gibbens and Prince (1963) found that in a London sample, two-thirds of the child victims had participated in indecencies on more than one occasion or with more than one assailant, and in a study in the United States two-thirds were considered to have been actively participating victims. Adults should take careful note of these figures, since the penalties are severe and the criminal population in English gaols does not take kindly to the presence of such offenders in their midst. Paedophilia is no more common amongst homosexual adults than it is amongst heterosexual adults, though this does not apply to the seduction of youths in the over-sixteen age-group.

Swanson (1968) quotes that in the majority of cases, the men are impotent and feel inadequate in approaching a full-grown woman. In his study, 48 percent were previously married, 28 percent single and 24 percent married with a spouse. In 56 percent, heterosexual adult adjustment was inadequate, 24 percent had a history of other sexual deviation and 20 percent appeared adequately heterosexually adjusted. In 56 percent of cases, the offender was experiencing conflict or loss of his usual source of sexual gratification. The offence may occur in person with widely varying personality structures and psychiatric diagnoses. Only one in four is what might be called the classical paedophiliac, i.e. having a specific sexual fixation on children. Often the sexual activity with the child is a replacement for a preferred adult sexual object.

The legal age of consent in England for females to engage in sexual activity is sixteen. Thus, technically, any sexual touching of a fifteen-year-old girl by a male could be considered illegal, an unhappy thought for a sixteen-year-old teen-age youth who indulges in petting with his girlfriend who is a year his junior. The age of consent for homosexual activity between males in England is twenty-one; thus, a twenty-year-old who partakes in any sexual activity of this type is still deemed a child and is acting illegally. Furthermore, his male partner, if twenty-two or over, could in theory become the victim of severe penalties through the courts. While such laws are no doubt designed to prevent the abuse of minors, such an age limit seems curious when one reflects that homosexual activity between adolescent males is commonplace and usually predates heterosexual activity. Furthermore, it is recognized as a normal phase of sexual development. Many non-western cultures look with curiosity at an apparently mature and intelligent society that can send otherwise respected citizens to gaol for what, to the unbiased and impartial observer, must be in most cases a very harmless piece of titillation which hurts no-one. As we have remarked in our chapter on homosexuality, there is no evidence to suggest that such activity, certainly in adolescence, has any type of harmful after-effect whatsoever.

The deviant paedophiliac, by our definition, is an individual who is sexually attracted to younger children. Often such individuals who come to the notice of the courts are relatives of the child in question; the offence is far more commonly seen amongst males than females. Most such men feel sexually inadequate and unable to make a mature relationship with another adult. The activity may be homosexual or heterosexual, or it may be an extension of narcissistic auto-eroticism, where the child is required by the adult to handle the adult's genitalia or masturbate him. Such an adult sees a relationship with a child as being less threatening and is able to obtain sexual arousal because in such a circumstance he does not feel inferior. They frequently suffer from impotence in an adult situation, and in many of the cases that come to light, the relationship has been in other respects a loving one where no threat has been intended to the child, though the child may have been bribed by an offer of money or candies. Often the ensuing publicity of the court case does more harm to the child than the original activity which, if not entirely enjoyed, was at least seen by the child in quite a different light from that in which adults would interpret it.

Unfortunately, this is not always the case. Children approached by strangers, for example in a public park or toilet, may feel much more threatened, and indeed actual assault may take place. Such cases fall under a different category and are in this sense much more perverse. Often such adults are of relatively low intelligence but in some cases the condition arises in an otherwise normal male whose heterosexual activities with his more usual partner have been temporarily brought to a halt, perhaps due to illness or pregnancy.

Treatment depends upon the total assessment of the case. Occasionally, such perverse sexual activity may arise as the result

of damage to frontal lobe circuits from injury or tumour. This
may need to be eliminated in the initial investigation.

Treatment programmes thereafter revolve principally around
psychotherapy and behaviour therapy of the aversion type.

Aversion therapy has come in for some criticism in recent
years from sociological groups who see the treatment as a brain-
washing procedure. To the author's mind, this implies a lack
of understanding of the technique, which is not basically coer-
cive. The principles are based on learning theory, and the co-
operation of the patient is essential for its effectiveness.

Learning theory basically consists of the following precepts.
If an organism feels a need, such as hunger, and a stimulus in
the shape of food is provided for it, then it will respond by con-
suming the food. Since it is rewarded in this process by the relief
of the need through gratification of the hunger, then the response
will become a learned pattern of behaviour and the organism
will tend to repeat this particular process under the same set of
circumstances in the future.

If what the organism consumes is in fact toxic and unpleasant to the palate and causes vomiting, then the need will not
have been satisfied and a negative conditioning or learning of
avoidance behaviour will take place.

This process can be applied to a wide variety of needs and
appears to be a general truth in most species studied. Thus, the
need may be hunger or thirst or it may apply to sexual drive or
a wide variety of socially determined factors in human society.
The development of anxiety can also be looked upon in this light
since anxiety avoidance is in itself a drive. Thus the organism
which is feeling anxious or fearful and responds to some stimulus in a way which reduces the level of fear will learn such a pattern of behaviour so that a reaction pattern as found in phobic
states may become a conditioned behavioural response.

Some patterns of behaviour are learned in this way because of
their immediate gratifying effect, but they may have longer-term
damaging implications to the individual. This is the case with
such things as alcoholism, where the immediate effect of taking
alcohol may be to satisfy a need and can be seen in stimulus re-

sponse theory terms. The anxiety-reducing effect of the alcohol at the time induces a conditioned response pattern, and the individual becomes dependent upon this behaviour, yet in the long term such an individual is aware of the dangers of alcoholism and the damage that he is doing to his health. Unfortunately, the immediate effect of gratification of need is stronger than the fear of long-term dangers. Thus, emphasizing the latter to such a patient is unlikely to be effective in relieving the former pattern of behaviour.

In aversion therapy, an attempt is made to break the cycle in the stimulus response system by intervening at the point where the organism's response gratifies and reinforces this reaction to the need. If the effects of drinking alcohol could be made unpleasant, for instance by using Antabuse® so that the individual felt ill and vomited after ingesting alcohol rather than feeling relaxed, then the habit-forming aspects of alcohol intake might be relieved. Positive psychotherapy thereafter directed towards encouraging alternative support systems that are not damaging to the health of the individual can then be more effectively procured.

Developments in the field of aversion therapy have led to the use of electrical aversion stimuli to the arm or hand of the patient, giving full control of the intensity of the pain response, its onset and its duration. Since these factors are of great importance in conditioning and deconditioning processes, their effective control in this manner makes treatment much more reliable than it would using Antabuse for alcoholics. The administration of the painful stimulus can be done by the therapist or by the patients themselves once they have learnt the technique; to be effective the intensity of the shock must be sufficiently strong to cause discomfort without being so intense as to cause the patient to give up the treatment altogether. Since pain is a subjective phenomenon, the control of this level must be left to the patient who is, of course, free to cheat or to lower the intensity to a degree which is no longer effective. Under such circumstances treatment will not be effective either, but the decision in such a matter lies firmly with the patient and in no way can be compared to a brain-washing technique.

In order to apply such techniques to the treatment of paedophilia, the patient is required to devise a hierarchy of erotic stimuli reinforced by slides or photographs or anything that could increase the fantasy. He fixes his attention on visualizing a scene with someone to whom he is attracted, and when the visual image is clear in his mind, the electric shock is applied. The patient continues to attempt to visualize this scene, which will gradually become more difficult for him to do. When this particular fantasy has been extinguished, the patient moves on through the hierarchy. This description is somewhat over-simplified; more sophisticated techniques can be employed to reinforce the aversive effect. The patient can utilize a portable battery-driven shock-box in order to continue the treatment on his own at home and in situations and circumstances which have previously reinforced the paedophiliac behaviour patterns.

This treatment in itself has obvious limitations but has nevertheless been shown to be effective in a variety of deviant behaviour patterns, not only in the sexual field.

At the same time, as has been mentioned above, psychotherapy designed to give positive help to the individual in order to develop a more mature stable relationship with adult females is carried out. Group therapy may be employed. The essence of therapy is to aid in the maturing process.

Exhibitionism and Voyeurism

The need to display is almost universal. It extends from the brilliant colouring of birds, fishes, insects, and even some parts of the vegetable kingdom to the courting and mating rituals of many mammal species. It is a normal pattern of human behaviour that sexual display, though subtly modified, is an important part of any pre-coital contact.

Normal display patterns are present in both male and female in the majority of species. In ape colonies, the pattern is often for the female to exhibit to the male in a provocative manner. This in turn excites the male, who responds to the female coquettishness by initiating pre-coital behaviour, which in turn excites the female so that she becomes sexually ready for coitus. Mating can then take place to the satisfaction of both.

Human behaviour follows similar patterns, though there is more cultural overlay modifying the basic behaviour. As a rule, although it is equally explicit, except in primitive communities, it has greater sophistication than that shown by apes.

By subtle provocation, the female human indicates to the male who is attracted to her that she would welcome further advances. The exhibition of this receptiveness towards the male, who is in this sense an onlooker or voyeur at the time, provokes a sexual response from him; his actions will in turn lead to female arousal.

The male tends to be aroused, therefore, by what he sees, and the female by a tactile stimulus, i.e. what is done to her. This is reflected in substitute patterns of sexual behaviour in humans, where male pornography generally has a visual impact and there is ready access to strip-tease shows, which are mostly by females designed for males. The counterpart of this in the female is the emphasis on sensuous tactile experiences through make-up and the materials with which female undergarments are made.

Thus, an element of exhibitionism and voyeurism is innate and necessary as a normal part of the process of attraction between the sexes.

In deviant exhibitionist or voyeuristic behaviour, the normal function of such activity is displaced and becomes an end in itself, without which arousal to climax may be impossible.

One should not view such patterns as an all-or-none thing, however. Many people find deviant outlets desirable or necessary at times but are perfectly capable of carrying on normal sexual activity at others. Indeed, the search for variety in such personalities is probably the dominant feature where it is a need for novelty in order to maintain a reasonable level of sexual arousal that is the most important factor.

The incidence of exhibitionism and voyeurism is difficult to estimate since it is only when such behaviour extends into illegal areas that it comes to people's notice. This may partly explain the apparently higher incidence in males, since females are more likely to find such overt behaviour threatening, and legal sanctions are therefore likely to be applied to the male.

Exhibitionism applies more specifically to behaviour in which the genitalia are exposed to bring gratification to the one who does the exposing. In fact, the obtaining of some mild sexual satisfaction by displaying one's sexual areas is extremely common in ordinary courting behaviour, particularly in females, where the recognition of the response this produces in their male partner is an added erotic stimulus. Such behaviour is acceptable in public display on the stage in many states, allowing any woman who does obtain a thrill from such behaviour patterns to indulge herself and get paid in the process. This opportunity is much less available for males.

The male who displays publicly in such a fashion is likely to fall foul of the law if a complaint is made. Prosecution may be under such laws designed to prevent a breach of the peace or more specifically the "making a lewd display." Court appearances for such offences are common, and figures quoted in Britain show some 3,000 cases are prosecuted annually.

Males involved in such behaviour are usually of somewhat immature or inadequate personality. They find great difficulty in developing mature adult sexual relationships. They are not usually dangerous in the sense that there is a risk to the female of rape, but are rather shy, introverted individuals who are unable to develop close personal contacts.

Exposeurs often need a slight element of risk if the exercise is to be sufficiently arousing. They usually expose to women who are alone and thereby obtain an erection, which may then be used for maturbatory purposes. The arousing of anxiety or sexual response in the woman is an added bonus but is often relatively unnecessary. In those who can afford it, prostitutes may serve as an outlet for such behaviour by allowing the man to adopt such patterns of behaviour in their presence, the fact that there is a financial contract removing the anxiety which a personal relationship produces and which evokes the impotence that the man fears with other women.

In some men, exhibitionism becomes a conditioned response which is their only way of obtaining satisfactory sexual relief. While aversion therapy may be effective in such individuals in removing the desire to exhibit, and drugs to reduce sexual drive may be employed in recidivist cases, these lines of therapy are negative and less likely to be effective than if combined with some positive attempt at maturing the personality and helping the man to overcome the anxieties which adult heterosexual activity, or the thoughts of it, produce.

In some individuals exhibitionism develops as a temporary pattern of behaviour when other sexual activity is denied; here the prognosis is obviously better if normal sexual behaviour is likely to be restored later.

Voyeurism usually refers to the obtaining of sexual arousal through watching the sexual activities of others but can be extended to include the illicit watching of others who are not specifically indulging in sexual activity, such as when undressing in a bedroom. Such individuals may be prosecuted in Britain under a very old law known commonly as the Peeping Tom Act. Other locations may prosecute under a breach of the peace or in some states specific laws designed to deal with the sexual aspects.

Such individuals who come to court are usually charged with having been caught looking through lighted windows or hiding themselves in places where they can observe women or couples in private situations. Again, this may be the only form of sexual release such an individual finds satisfying, but it is actually only a perverted extension of the normal eroticism which most would feel if observing such activity. Again, the strip-tease show caters to such needs, and prostitutes may provide the opportunity for individuals to observe her working with other clients, again for a fee. The voyeur may combine the viewing of sexual activity with masturbation. It is much more commonly found in the male, who is likely to be aroused more by sexual visual stimuli than the female, though one famous example is Mary, Countess of Pembroke, who in John Aubrey's novel is described as "having a contrivance that in the Spring of the year when the stallions were to meet the mares they were to be brought before such a part of the house where she had a vedette to look on them and please herself of their sport, and then she would act the like sport herself with her stallions."

Strip-tease shows are a popular and acceptable method for many individuals to obtain voyeuristic gratification to a minor degree, but in Britain a convicted peeping tom may be bound over to keep the peace, and in some states of the United States they are liable to imprisonment.

Exhibitionism is the commonest deviation to come into conflict with the law and therefore with the medical practitioner. In 1954, 2,728 persons were convicted of this offence in Britain, and of 1,985 sexual offenders studied by the Cambridge Department of Criminal Science, 490 were classified as having committed some form of indecent exposure. Follow-up studies show that within four years, 19 percent had been reconvicted. Prosecution occurs under the Vagrancy Act of 1824, which provides that every person "wilfully, openly, ludely and obscenely exposing his person with intent to insult any female is a rogue and vagabond."

Fetishism

Specific objects or situations may become incorporated into patterns of sexual behaviour. Mechanisms of imprinting may play a part, since not infrequently the particular fetishistic object appears to have been chosen through coincidental circumstances producing arousal at critical stages in the development of sexual activity in such individuals. Later, such an individual may find that the ability to become aroused at all depends on this particular object or circumstance being available and without which impotence or frigidity may be present.

Fetishism therefore is the term used to describe the condition in which this pattern of behaviour becomes necessary to normal sexual functioning. Such behaviour is usually harmless and is unlikely to come the way of courts. An exception to this, perhaps, is where individuals resort to theft in order to satisfy a fetish. The need for a particular object may become a compulsion, and such individuals may collect vast numbers of ladies' panties, for example. If they steal these from clothes-line rather than buying them, then they may eventually come the way of the police who, if they search the house, may find vast numbers of apparently unused such articles in the individual's possession. The use of such objects as an aid to masturbation may have been expanded to the point where masturbation no longer becomes a necessary part. Some sublimation presumably occurs, and the collecting of the articles then becomes an end in itself. Such cases are rare, however, and the majority of fetishists openly consult their doctors if their partners find their behaviour unacceptable, so that help is requested.

A considerable element of fantasy comes into fetishistic behaviour. Certain objects particularly seem to be utilized. These are silky materials such as commonly used in female underwear, clothing made of leather or rubber, and specific articles such as shoes or hair. To consider fetishism just on the basis of those requiring this type of article, however, is to take a rather narrow view. Certainly in this narrow view, the condition appears much commoner in males. If we broaden the concept, however, to encompass not just a fixation upon particular articles which act in this sense as sexual aids, but rather include special conditions which act as aids when the "object" in this sense is a behaviour pattern such as fixation on fellatio (oral sex female to male) or cunnilingus (oral sex male or female) or to anal sex, sex with animals, triolism (threesome sexual activities) and narcissism where the do-it-yourself aspect leads to solitary masturbation in which aids may be incorporated, then the whole concept of deviancy is a much broader one. While strictly speaking much of this is not fetishism, it is in the author's view another aspect of the same thing where the prime need is originality of experience. Where the individual finds that particular behaviour patterns are more erotic, sexual behaviour thereafter becomes fixated on this type of response.

Taking this broader concept, it is undoubtedly the case that many women are able to obtain arousal to climax only when special conditions operate. This may relate to the heightened stimulation produced by vibrators, through use of oral sex or to particular conditions which need to be present or which need to operate in the pre-coital phase if arousal is to reach a sufficient level of intensity. Climax then becomes impossible unless these circumstances are met.

In women, the emphasis again is different from the behaviour patterns in men, no doubt for the reasons outlined above, namely, more emphasis on tactile than on visual stimuli and the tendency for romanticism to be the female equivalent of pornography. Seen in this light, the ability to induce erotic thoughts should be no more or no less acceptable in either sex using whatever method is appropriate to that sex. Perhaps we must make a distinction between the abnormal sex portrayed in "hard porn" magazines illustrating deviant behaviour as opposed to "soft porn," where explicit sexual acts between couples are all that is displayed. Looked at intellectually, there seems little difference in the final effect, though most juries would consider that the portrayal of illegal acts was calculated to corrupt and deprave, whereas the over-romanticized short story was an example of moral virtue. This simply indicates that what turns females on is considered more socially acceptable than what turns males on in this supposedly male-dominated society.

The sex difference is by no means an exclusive one; there is considerable overlap. Many individuals of both sexes find the portrayal of abnormal sexual activity (in the accepted sense as opposed to the statistical one) abhorrent. The argument for its suppression lies in the possibility that the depiction and reminding of individuals that such acts can take place may encourage more frequent adoption of such behaviour. Others, however, including such researchers as Yaffé in London (1973), have argued that the scanning of such literature acts as a sublimation and decreases the risk of violent perverted behaviour in the community.

There seems little logic in attempting to treat mild fetishistic behaviour. Fetishism is only likely to cause a problem if one partner finds the other partner's sexual needs distasteful. On the one side, reassurance and perhaps a broadening of the horizons of one partner may be helpful, while in the other partner, advice to pay more consideration towards their partner's likes and dislikes and not to impose things which are distasteful may be the best line to adopt. It is often worth pointing out that such behaviour, while being a matter of taste, is usually harmless. If one partner is unable to function effectively in a sexual role without a fetishistic element being introduced, then surely both will be better satisfied if that partner is able to perform as a result than if one is rendered impotent or frigid, in which case no-one is the beneficary.

Prostitutes are well aware of these needs in their clients and cater extensively to them. Virtually all aspects of sexual behaviour have their market; many prostitutes specialize in providing facilities for cross-dressing or unusual articles of clothing, rubber-wear, leather-wear and particular types of sexual practice. Thus, in Britain, ladies who advertise that they have O-levels or A-levels are indicating that oral or anal sex is acceptable to them.

Using our broader definition of fetishism, mild degrees of such behaviour are extremely commonplace between otherwise normal couples, and indeed such sexual behaviour is in every sense normal if it is part of a prelude to heterosexual mating. It is only when the behaviour becomes an end in itself that the term deviancy can really be applied to it.

We have listed the commoner fetishistic objects. Conditioned patterns of behaviour appear to be the only aetiological mechanisms that can be identified at present. Texture certainly seems to play a part in the materials so used, and some writers have suggested that the interest in rubber-wear, for example, relates to erotic experiences in infancy and early childhood associated with accidental stimulation to the genitals during washing or changing or to erotic stimuli associated with visual imagery in early puberty. This does not seem entirely satisfactory since it does not explain sex differences nor is it relevant to the introjective qualities of transvestism and the attraction to leather-wear. Similarly, controlled trials would be unlikely to show that those who possess fetishistic preoccupations had any significantly different early upbringing from those who do not, although the author is not aware that any such controlled trial has actually been performed.

It is possible that the first orgasmic experiences of the adolescent often masturbatory in nature, may be highly significant and that articles or events associated with these early experiences have imprinting value in the same way as in other species and akin to the attachment behaviour causing pair-bonding. It is difficult, however, to obtain clear-cut histories which might suggest this; much of the material must needs be anecdotal.

Sado-Masochism

Sadism is the term used to describe sexual deviation in which erotic excitement is derived from the infliction of pain. *Masochism* refers to the deviation in which sexual pleasure is aroused by the reception of pain. However, the words are often combined since it is commonly found that the two go together in one individual. But even if not in one individual, then the two usually go together in any partnership arrangements.

Indeed, the two attitudes were combined in those two individuals from whom the names are derived — the Marquis de Sade and the Chevalier Leopold von Sacher-Masoch. De Sade was primarily concerned with domination and infliction of pain, whereas Sacher-Masoch gained satisfaction from being subjugated and beaten. Sacher-Masoch was also a fetishist interested in fur; de Sade was fascinated by sodomy. And as both were prolific writers, we have obtained considerable knowledge of these syndromes from their literary offerings.

Pornographic literature is commonly devoted to sado-masochistic pursuits, and the kinkier dating magazines contain plenty of opportunities for those who wish to indulge. To those who do not have this particular interest, however, the connection between sexual gratification and the inflicting or receiving of pain is incomprehensible. Milder degrees of sado-masochism in the shape of humiliation, bondage and the application of certain types of transvestite behaviour in group situations are not uncommon, however, and are often employed by prostitutes for clients who cannot obtain this kind of satisfaction in their normal lives. Whether the relationship is a psychological one or whether it has some sort of physiological basis, as some aspects of research into brain function may suggest, is not clear. To some extent, the condition may be the result of an early conditioning imprinting experience.

Many couples engage in minor sado-masochistic rituals which serve the purpose of arousing them erotically and are introductory steps to the act itself. It is only when sado-masochism is extreme or divorced from intercourse that it can be counted as a deviation, and it is in these cases that extraordinary lengths may be taken to effect gratification. Many mildly passive males, however, enjoy the domination of a woman in the sexual field; as this is foreign to the majority of female attitudes, the individual may again need to resort to prostitutes to obtain this kind of gratification. There is commonly an element of this in the rituals found associated with modern witchcraft, black magic and some of the group sexual activities which take place in the metropolises.

The association of pain with sexual arousal is a curious one, although when one recalls the mating patterns of many species, the similarity between the aggressive behaviour the male exhibits to other males and the courting behaviour the male exhibits to the female is quite striking. Correspondingly, female responses to the male are often comparable to the response the non-dominant male makes when wishing to avoid an aggressive attack by a more dominant member of the species. This work has been well documented in *Naked Ape* by Desmond Morris (1968).

As with much deviant behaviour, the presence of minor degrees of sado-masochistic experience are commonplace between humans during normal mating procedures. Often when an individual is highly aroused, the administration of what would in the non-aroused state be a painful stimulus may in fact increase arousal and be experienced as erotic.

Again, like many deviant activities, the presence of sadism in isolation or masochism in isolation is rarely found. Much more commonly, such practices are interchangeable between the individuals and are only part of a more deviant pattern of sexual behaviour.

Furthermore, the infliction or receipt of physical pain is but

not wish to go to this degree of degradation but prefer to be forced into a submissive role, where they may act out as a maid at a party or serve as the recipient of group sexual activity or simply accept orders from the prostitute to do such things as cleaning or washing up within the apartment. Again the need seems to be for wide variety, and the more imaginative the partner can be, the better the effect for the client. Some individuals may only be able to function knowing that the partner has indulged in sexual practices or intercourse with others, hence the appeal of the prostitute in such cases. Some, however, may require their ordinary partners to have intercourse with another person in their presence in order that they themselves become aroused. Still others like to wear soiled clothing which has been used by prostitutes, and the kinky dating journals seem to have a good market in the advertising of soiled panties for sale. This anonymous kind of fetishistic behaviour is incorporated into masturbatory rituals. The masochistic element in such behaviour patterns is clear.

Sadistic behaviour of a more perverse kind and dangerous to the recipient is seen in some of the more macabre crimes of necrophilia and sexually motivated murders. Crimes of rape also fall into this category. Individuals who take part in these deviancies usually show a more marked personality disturbance of psychopathic type or may suffer psychotic delusions. Such problems usually come the way of special hospitals and of course are in quite a different category from the minor deviant behaviour that has been outlined above.

The practitioner confronted with cases of sado-masochistic behaviour where advice is sought must weigh from the evidence whether treatment is merited or justified. In the bulk of cases, reassurance is all that is appropriate. Marital counselling may be desirable, and in the more serious cases, recourse to aversion therapy with appropriate positive support in developing mature relationships may be embarked upon. This has been described in an earlier section.

In the author's view, the bulk of deviancy problems are trivial and are not within the remit of medical practice. Better sexual education and the development by society of more tolerant attitudes as has been seen in some Scandinavian countries is likely to put such problems in more sensible perspective, since most of such behaviour is a harmless amusement. It is only when others are involved unwillingly that society seems to need recourse to the law. The application of many laws relating to sexual practice is archaic and their revision would seem to be timely.

Other Deviancies

PORNOGRAPHY. The word *pornography* derives from the Greek and literally means "writing concerning prostitutes" but in effect has come to mean the expression of deviancy in literature or art. Thus, while not strictly in itself an example of deviancy, it is closely associated with those groups where exceptional partners or conditions are required for satisfactory sexual arousal. Hyde (1964) has written a history of pornography which shows that this, more than any other example of deviant thinking and behaviour, is subject to marked variation in fashion and in gross absurdities in the law. An example is quoted of a man found guilty in 1895 of sending pornographic material through the mail, the material in question, in fact, being a quotation from the Bible. The subject is reviewed more recently by Yaffé (1973) in the *British Journal of Hospital Medicine*. Yaffé concludes that there is no evidence that pornography has any effect on sexual behaviour, the majority of people being exposed to pornographic material at some time but only a minority engaging in illegal deviant practices. A useful review of the literature is given in the references.

Stoller (1970) discusses the relationship between pornography and perversion and states that, "Pornography is a day-dream in which activities usually, but not necessarily, overtly sexual are projected into written or pictorial material to induce genital excitement in an observer." Pornography is for restitution. Men are the main producers and consumers. "Its creation and its use are ritualised acts, for deviation from a narrow prescribed path will produce decreased sexual excitement. At these moments it reveals the function of perversion as a necessary preserver of potency."

PROSTITUTION. A *prostitute* is defined as an individual who indiscriminately provides sexual relations in return for monetary payment, the principal point being the casual and promiscuous relationship. It is, however, impractical to confine the term to those persons who derive their entire living from prostitution, since a large number of females who engage in such activities do so as an adjunct to a regular occupation. The condition is generally confined to females, possibly for social reasons, but also by virtue of the fact that the male is unable to obtain sexual arousal necessary to perform such a function with the regularity that is required. Nevertheless, their usage is largely confined to the male, and the problem must, therefore, be considered from two viewpoints, that of the female who engages in such trade and that of the male who employs her.

Kinsey defines four types of prostitution, the commonest involving heterosexual relations for which the female is paid. There is also homosexual prostitution between males where the receiver usually offers fellatio or anal intercourse. Thirdly, there is a small group of heterosexual prostitutes in which the female pays the male. And the rarest of the four types involves females who are paid for homosexual relations which they supply to other females.

The kind of services offered varies within the social structure of the society in which it is plied. For example, masseuses employed in the more offbeat massage establishments in bigger cities may offer a complete massage which includes masturbation of the client for an additional fee, though these individuals would probably be shocked at the suggestion that they should take their services to the extent of complete intercourse.

Kinsey states that some 69 percent of the total male white population in their series had had experience at some time with prostitutes. Commonly, however, this was a single experience, and not more than 15 to 20 percent had had regular contacts. Prostitution accounts for less than one-tenth of the total nonmarital outlet of the male population, and the incidence is said to have dropped significantly in recent years, perhaps as the need for them has also diminished. Kinsey gives a large number of references appertaining to the subject.

Men visit prostitutes because they can pay for the sex relations and forget other responsibilities. Normal involvement with a member of the opposite sex may have social implications beyond their inclination. The main importance of prostitutes in this country, however, is probably in the provision of an outlet for deviant sexual behaviour which the prostitute is prepared to supply for money and which the male may be unable to obtain elsewhere. Thus this gratification may prevent considerable problems from developing in a small sub-section of the community who might otherwise live in total frustration, acting out their problems in a more anti-social manner. Dating literature through such magazines as *Contak, His and Hers, Romeo and Juliet* and many others which spring up from time to time, including those specifically catering to homosexuals such as *Apollo* are full of advertisements from amateurs and professionals prepared to offer a wide variety of deviant services. With the suppression of street soliciting, this is the only medium through which such people can contact each other, the only possible legal risk being if their advertisement contravenes the law or if obscene material is sent through the post.

Particular techniques such as bondage, the making up of threesomes for triolism or couples wishing to join up for foursomes are also found. These contacts provide the interested deviant individual with the opportunity for indulging what would seem to many as perverted behaviour in a manner which is impersonal and lacking in individual responsibility. In such a way, the embarrassment of approaching a normal heterosexual partner with such a proposition, probably to the ruination of the relationship, can be avoided.

Some men go to prostitutes because they are ineffective in securing sexual relationships with other girls or occasionally because they are unable to perform satisfactorily in terms of erectile function with individuals for whom they have respect. The dangers, however, of contagious disease are obvious to those with medical training, though this is more likely to be encountered in willing amateurs than in professionals with a living to make.

Looking at this problem from the other angle, one may ask what the motive is that so many females are prepared to take up this particular trade. One obvious motivating factor is the simple one of wages, since the earnings of a successful lady in big cities may approach £10,000 ($20,000 to $30,000) per annum, and even "kinky" masseuses in sauna parlours can probably make £5,000 tax-free on the quiet. Nevertheless, this is probably not the only motivating factor, there also being a small number in whom eroticism may play a part and others in whom a certain fulfilment in terms of human contact of an uncommitted kind is satisfying. The League of Nations Study (1938) on prostitution found that between 20 and 30 percent of women adopting this life on a regular basis had lost one parent through death or separation while they were still young, and the percentage brought up in institutions, by foster-parents or by relatives was a further 20 percent more. Thus, emotional deprivation and insecure early relationships leading to other deviant behaviour in individuals may also lead the female into a life of prostitution, and in this sense it may be considered as a typically feminine aspect of deviant behaviour.

BUGGERY. Intercourse between a male and another male or female partner using the rectum as the recipient for the penis (sodomy) is commonly practised in certain situations but is for some reason harshly dealt with by the law. It is used commonly between homosexuals, the passive partner taking the female role, and in some sub-cultures between male and female as a means of contraception. The other form of buggery — bestiality — comprises relationships between a human and another species of animal and applies to intercourse whether through the anus or the vagina. This offence may be committed with either male or female taking an active role. Either way, it is illegal and comes in for severe legal sanctions logically beyond the seriousness of the act.

In order to qualify as a form of deviant behaviour, the practice would have to be indulged in as an end in itself as a replacement for normal heterosexual intercourse, even though circumstances made the latter a practical possibility. It is a felony for a person to commit buggery with another person or with an animal under the Sexual Offences Act of 1956 in Britain, and the punishment to which an offender is liable is life imprisonment. It remains a criminal offence even when the couple are husband and wife and each consents to the act. This farcical situation is made even more curious by the recognition that the anal area is erotically sensitive in some individuals; neuro-anatomical studies point to the reasons for this. Recent changes in the law have made the situation even more absurd since such action is now legal between consenting male adults in private, but still not between husband and wife.

TRIOLISM. Triolism, or the involvement of three individuals in a sexual union, again is widely available through the kinky magazines and obviously, therefore, supplies a fairly commonly felt need. The extension of threesomes into foursome wife-swapping parties and group orgies, not uncommon in some sub-cultures in our society, is not strictly speaking deviance nor indeed illegal, though it is worth noting that the current law in Britain allows two females to conduct a sexual display, in a club striptease act, for example, but two males may not. Similarly, a threesome may contain one man and two women but is not allowed to contain two men and one woman. Nor are males allowed to conduct a sexual display in public even though homosexual acts by consenting adults in private are now allowed. Homosexual acts by consenting adults in private are not even legal now if more than two are present or if an individual under age should be present. State laws in the United States are variable. The practitioner is, however, hardly likely to be requested to treat such problems, though he may well be required to attempt to pick up the pieces from broken marriages resulting from wife-swapping parties.

FROTTEURISM. Frotteurism is the practice of rubbing the genitalia against another person, usually undertaken in a crowd situation. The focus of interest is commonly the buttocks of the female, which is apt to be indulged in in a compulsive manner. It is seldom found as an isolated deviance and is of little importance except when a complaint is made so the individual finds himself in court. It is not always easy to disprove such an accusation, and the unfortunate offender may be convicted of indecent assault punishable by a sentence of two years imprisonment. In elderly people, it may be evidence of the loosening of morality which goes with an early dementing state.

RAPE. This condition hardly comes under the categories to be considered in this book but is mentioned for the sake of completeness, since the sexual relationship involved in a rape is heterosexual, the deviance stemming from the lack of consent by the victim, the relationship therefore being of a more vicious and criminal kind. A certain amount of aggression is a common precedence to intercourse in many animals and sometimes in humans, though not usually approaching "sexual intercourse by force or trickery," which is the legal definition of rape. This crime is said to be increasing despite the more permissive society, showing that rape is a much more complicated condition psychologically than one might anticipate. Indeed there are considered to be at least four types of rapist. The first is the man who is too timid to make approaches to a woman and feels inferior. The second type can only obtain sexual pleasure in violating a woman by force. Such men are true deviants and may be extremely dangerous. The third type, perhaps the commonest, is a man who commits rape in an impulsive manner; these are poorly controlled, immature men who under the influence of alcohol give way to sexual urges in an uncontrolled, anti-social manner. Many are psychopathic. The fourth group consists of those who are mentally ill, commonly with the diagnosis of schizophrenia or mild mental retardation. Perhaps a fifth group might be considered in the motorcycle clans who indulge in "gang bangs" where a group of males has forcible intercourse with a woman who may not always be initially unwilling.

The practitioner, who in police surgeon capacity, is confronted by a case of alleged rape should proceed with great caution; advice is given in this matter in most of the standard textbooks on legal medicine.

Those who are unable to make a personal relationship of any kind with another human being range from the bizarre and psychotic necrophiliac through pygmalionism and bestiality to the milder forms of auto-eroticism of fetishism and narcissism.

NECROPHILIA. This condition describes the individual who obtains sexual gratification by intercourse with a corpse. This is a bizarre and often psychotic condition but may be found in severe psychopathy. It is of little relevance to the medical profession except in defending the occasional murder case. The condition is extremely rare.

PYGMALIONISM. This condition has been discussed previously in this work but only in its historical context. Again, it is extremely rare and of little consequence. The condition describes those who derive sexual gratification from inanimate objects such as statues, perhaps its modern counterpart being in those individuals who obtain, as part of a masturbatory ritual, dummies, dolls or lifelike blow-up objects obtainable in the more bizarre sex stores with realistic artificial vaginas, or for the female, dildoes or artificial penises, available even with urethras which can produce a mimicked ejaculation.

BESTIALITY. This condition refers to sexual intercourse or activities of a sexual nature, either vaginal or anal with a species other than a human. In Britain, this comes within the Sexual Offences Act of 1956 as being a felony punishable by life imprisonment, as is sodomy. The condition as outlined earlier is found either in primitive farming communities or as a more bizarre variant in the kinky set among sophisticated prostitutes. Occasionally, individuals require this kind of stimulation in order to obtain sexual gratification for themselves. A case was seen of a man who required his wife to have intercourse with an Alsation dog while he, in a voyeur capacity, masturbated to orgasm. His wife tired of this and took a lover; the pair hatched a plot to get rid of the husband by accusing him of encouraging this act and made a complaint to the police. Unfortunately, the plot misfired as the lady had technically committed the more serious crime of buggery, her husband having merely aided and abetted.

This deviation seldom comes under the direct scrutiny of the psychiatrist, and perhaps the offence is more commonplace in fantasy than in fact. It is commoner among males and often is associated with photography, prostitutes being persuaded to indulge in such acts so that the male may obtain gratification by observing and photographing the events. The psychiatrist may be involved in the legal consequences arising therefrom.

NARCISSISM. The name of this condition derives from Narcissus, who fell in love with his own reflection in a pool. It refers to those individuals who find sexual satisfaction from masturbatory arousal, commonly in front of a mirror so that they can observe their own image in action. It is, in fact, commonplace for people to enjoy watching themselves during the course of normal sexual activity, and masturbation is commonplace in the majority of the adolescent population and at other times when normal outlets are not available. As an end in itself, however, the condition may become deviant. These people occasionally advertise in the contact magazines as D.I.Y. (do-it-yourself) enthusiasts who wish to make contact with others of like interests.

Recent references from which further material may be obtained are as follows: *Sado-masochism,* by Shove, published in 1971; *Necrophilia,* by Gromska, published in 1969; *Rape,* by Robinson, published in 1971; *Fetishism,* by Zavitzianos, published in 1971; *Prostitution,* by Polenz and Deisher, published in 1970; and *Exhibitionism,* by Zachmeh, published in 1971.

Chapter 14

TREATMENT OF SEXUAL BEHAVIOURAL ANOMALIES

WHILE ONE CAN POSTULATE that sexually deviant people possess some genetic defect of a general kind which interferes with their capacity to reach emotional maturity or some biochemical determining factor in the case of some types of homosexuality, the majority of deviances demonstrate a partial failure in the individual to achieve a fully adult sexual status. The histories of many argue a strong case for the condition being attributable to imprinting.

Treatment concepts fall into three general classes:

PSYCHOTHERAPY. This may be analytical in character, attempting to deal with the problems of the deviant in order to resolve them or, more probably, allowing the individual to come to terms with his problem and learn to live with it in a more mature manner, channelling his needs into socially acceptable forms.

AVERSION THERAPY. Many of the minor deviancies such as fetishism or offences which may come through the courts such as paedophilia lend themselves admirably to deconditioning processes using learning therapy principles and the elaboration of some type of electrical aversion therapy applied to their particular problem, in reality or in imagination, using stimulus-response procedures.

THE USE OF DRUGS. This implies the use of phenothiazines, anti-depressants or anxiolytics in appropriate circumstances and occasionally the use of hormone therapy, in particular cyproterone and the butyrophenone benperidol.

These are all specialist procedures which require referral to an appropriate clinic. Straightforward counselling, however, by the patient's general practitioner may be all that is necessary in many cases since the alleviation of guilt through understanding of the problems involved and education of the individual may be all that is required.

Motivation is an important factor in the treatment of any condition. This makes self-referral an important feature in assessing prognosis, since cases that come through the courts or for which court procedures are threatened are likely to come not because they wish for a change in their behaviour, but because of fear of the consequences of their actions. West goes into the details of methods of treatment and gives a large number of references, principally with regard to treatment of homosexuality. Authorities are divided on the success of treatment for this condition, but the results may well reflect the fact that the condition is not an homogenous entity.

Some psychiatrists have expressed the view that the chances of cure in confirmed cases are negligible and that the psychiatrist should concentrate on making the patient a better adjusted homosexual rather than aspiring to conversion. Those authorities who believe homosexuality to be a genetically fixed condition contend that attempts to attack it are futile and unjustified. Nevertheless, in those cases, particularly in the young, where a bisexual pattern of behaviour is evidenced, aversion therapy directed against the homosexual inclination combined with positive therapy designed to remove heterosexual fears has achieved considerable success, according to some authorities.

In considering treatment for any individual case, the aims must be identified and either supportive psychotherapy or behaviourist-oriented procedures considered and outlined to the patient.

With regard to drugs, it has been shown that androgenic hormones stimulate sex desire without altering direction of sexual interest. Oestrogens may afford some protection from impulsive and foolhardy sexual exploits in damping down sexual drive in the male. Transsexual patients may attempt to obtain oestrogens in order to effect further conversion towards the female form, but in general terms, this is probably best resisted unless the prospect of sex change operation is seriously being considered. Castration has been used in Denmark for convicted sex criminals who have been pronounced psychopathic and committed to prison on this basis. They are able to obtain quicker release by volunteering to undergo the operation. The ablation of certain areas of the brain has also been attempted, and some success has been claimed in cases of aggressive sexual behaviour.

In his final chapter, West (1976) suggests prevention by tolerance. "No known method of treatment or punishment offers hope of making any substantial reduction of the vast army of adults practising homosexuality. Rather than by pretending they don't exist or hoping to eradicate them by sheer weight of disapproval it would be more realistic to try and find room for them in society so that they can live unmolested and make their contribution to the common good."

Particular methods of treatment in homosexuality have been discussed in numerous articles in the journals. Ovesey (1954) discusses the analysis of homosexual conflict and points out that not only sexual problems need to be treated, but also the neurosis related to power and dependancy.

Behaviour therapy for sexual disorders is discussed by Dengrove (1967). This type of therapy is also considered appropriate for transvestism, exhibitionism and other sexual deviations such as voyeurism and narcissism. Raymond (1969), in discussing aversion therapy for sexual deviations, states that homosexuality is not markedly influenced by aversion therapy but that the procedure is useful in exhibitionism and fetishism. Bancroft (1969) also finds that aversion therapy produces poor results in homosexuality (also Bancroft 1975).

Marks, Gelder and Bancroft (1970) followed up the results of electric aversion therapy two years after treatment in a group of twenty-four patients with transvestism, fetishism and sadomasochism. They discussed the prognostic indicators and gave further references with regard to the treatment of these conditions. They found that deviant activities diminished considerably. Improvement was maintained throughout follow-up in most cases despite minor relapses. Improvement was transient or absent in patients who had strong transsexual feelings. Improvement usually occurred early in treatment, and a control group who remained untreated changed less during the follow-up period. They concluded that electrical aversion therapy produced worthwhile improvement in most patients but had to be part of a careful plan of clinical management.

The hormonal treatment of sexual offenders is considered by Field and Williams (1970), where the treatment of imprisoned sexual offenders with female hormone indicated that this approach might be of value in those sexual offenders considered unsuitable for other methods of treatment. They note that Dunn (1940) had succeeded in achieving complete loss of libido with treatment by oral stilboestrol and that this might be of value in habitual sexual offenders. Stilboestrol, 5 mg per day by mouth for two weeks, has produced the cessation of activity and fantasies within ten days according to Whittaker (1959). By eliminating sexual reinforcement, competing social reinforcers are strengthened as a side-effect. Implants allow a period during which there is an increased probability of the patient's behaviour coming under the control of normal social reinforcers with consequent development of behaviour incompatible with the deviant behaviour.

Other drugs that have more recently been introduced include a butyrophenone which suppress abnormal sexuality called benperidol. It is said to reduce fantasy rather than abolish potency. Cyproterone acetate, an anti-androgen that acts on the pituitary gland, has a castrating effect without feminising. There appears to be hope, therefore, that in the not too distant future, further drugs may be developed which can act as aids in this respect. In the meantime, the treatment of homosexuality probably lies on the lines of supportive psychotherapy in most cases, whereas those with specific deviations are treated successfully at present with electrical aversion techniques.

Chapter 15

MEDICO-LEGAL CONCEPTS

IN MANY CIVILISED countries, homosexual behaviour does not
contravene the law except in special circumstances of abuse,
for instance, if children are involved or if force is used. But in
other places, as in some states in the United States, any kind of
sexual contact between persons of the same sex counts as a serious crime. This is reviewed in West's (1976) book.

The laws governing sexual conduct descend directly from
ancient religious codes. In ancient times, Jewish religious institutions included the *kadash* or male homosexual temple prosti
tute. The Old Testament makes no mention of lesbianism, but
St. Paul condemns women who lust after one another and give
themselves up to vile passions (Rom. 1:26). The Christian
church adopted the ancient Jewish sex codes and formalised them
into ecclesiastical laws which later provided the basis for English common law. In mediaeval times, when clerical preoccupa-
tion with sins of the flesh was at its height, many men and women
were sent to their deaths for homosexual offences. Even married persons were not immune, for confessors were supplied with
instruction manuals to ensure that intercourse took place only
in the approved position. Sexual perversions flourished in this
repressive atmosphere, and the religious books of the time describe at great length and in great detail every conceivable sexual aberration, giving appropriate penalties for each sin.

West reviews the laws in different countries in order to make
the point that most are illogical and depend on the social cli-
mate at the time the law is introduced.

The model penal code prepared by the American Law Institute has provided that private sexual acts should be criminal only where minors are involved or some force or coercion is used. Since 1962 this reform has been put into effect in Illinois and more recently in other states. It is, however, still a criminal offence to commit adultery in the state of New York.

Muslim law condemns homosexual acts; in the ancient Muslim religious code, sodomy and adultery were both serious offences punishable by death. In Pakistan, adultery is a criminal offence, and although some forms of homosexual behaviour are permitted, sodomy is punished severely.

In England, homosexual crimes first became a matter for secular courts in 1533 when a statute was introduced under Henry VIII making sodomy punishable by death. It remained so until the nineteenth century when it was reduced to life imprisonment. The Offences Against the Person Act of 1861, Section 61, which remained in force until 1956, reads: "Whoever shall be convicted of the abominable crime of buggery committed either with mankind or with any animal shall be liable at the discretion of the Court to imprisonment for life."

Under the Criminal Law Amendment Act of 1885, sexual acts between males of any age became offences of gross indecency. More recently, the 1965 Sexual Offences Act defined rape, inecst, unnatural offences, indecent assault and gross indecency, and three types of unlawful intercourse involving females under the age of 16, females under the age 13, and with mental defectives at any age. A further Act of importance was the 1960 Indecency With Children Act, whereby it was an offence to persuade a child to handle an adult indecently. Under the 1965 Act, any sexual touching of a child of either sex under the age of sixteen was defined and punished as indecent assault regardless of whether the child resisted or encouraged. But the maximum penalties differed, being two years imprisonment if the victim was a girl and ten years if a boy. When intercourse takes place with a girl under age, the law distinguishes between child victims of twelve or under, for which the maximum penalty is life imprisonment, and victims under 16 where the maximum penalty is two years. No such distinction occurs in the case of homosexual activities with boys, where the maximum penalty remains life imprisonment for sodomy. Gross indecency under the Act was not defined, but the Court of Criminal Appeal has held that it is not even necessary for men to touch each other, since indecent exhibiting to one another in public is sufficient. It is also an offence under Section 32 for a man persistently to solicit or importune in a public place for immoral purposes.

Following upon the Wolfenden Report, a new Sexual Offences Act was established in Britain in 1967. This removed the legal penalties for homosexual acts in private between men over twenty-one and removed the anomaly whereby anal contacts carried more severe penalties than other kinds of intercourse. As with female prostitution, the individual private transaction is not, therefore, now illegal, except with those under twenty-one years of age, or in public (which means if more than two persons are present), or if consent is not obtained. All types of homosexual acts committed by men over twenty-one with youths of sixteen to twenty-one, even though the youth participates willingly, may incur a penalty of up to five years imprisonment for the older man. Homosexual acts with boys under sixteen continue to have the existing penalties. Homosexual acts committed by a youth under twenty-one with a consenting partner of any age over sixteen may incur a penalty of up to two years imprisonment. But youths under twenty-one are not to be proceeded against without the consent of the Director of Public Prosecutions.

For further details of these Acts, the reader is referred to a textbook of legal medicine such as that of Gradwohl (1968). The law against rape, which cannot be dealt with in detail here, is also considered, and advice is given to the practitioner who is required to examine in such an alleged circumstance. A consideration of the psychiatric aspects of sexual offenders is given in the same book, where advice is given on how the practitioner should proceed when advising the court on such matters as the question of legal responsibility. The practitioner must be cautious while acting in a police surgeon capacity, for example, when he sees cases where evidence of deviancy is present, in particular where the victim is found asphyxiated and dressed in female

clothes. The likelihood of accidental death is probable. Accidental death may also occur in association with sado-masochistic
rituals, but it it is quite possible that the patient may have become the victim of an assault that went beyond the normal range
expected, which may incur a criminal charge of more severity.
Examination of the victim is an important skill. This is particularly so in cases of alleged sodomy, where examination of the anal
passage may be required. Gradwohl's textbook takes these points
in detail and advises on them.

Field and Williams (1970) reviewed the Sexual Offences Act
of 1967; the new penalties for gross indecency with a child under
age of fourteen punishable by imprisonment for two years, and
on summary convictions, six months imprisonment and/or a
fine of £100. Indecent assault on a girl under thirteen carries a
maximum sentence of imprisonment for five years, and two years
if the girl is over thirteen. Indecent assault on a boy under the
age of sixteen has a maximum sentence of ten years, while an attempt to have intercourse with a girl under the age of thirteen
carries with it imprisonment up to seven years. Intercourse itself can be punished by life imprisonment. Sexual intercourse
with a girl in the age-group thirteen to sixteen is liable to a maximum punishment of two years imprisonment. Buggery of a
consenting boy over the age of sixteen has a maximum imprisonment of five years; if the boy did not consent, the maximum sentence is ten years. Life imprisonment is the maximum sentence
if it involves a boy under the age of sixteen, and it is to be noted
that under that age a boy cannot legally consent to the act. Field
and Williams comment that it is not to be thought that life imprisonment for buggery or rape is all that rare. At the time of
writing, there were five men serving life sentences for offences
of buggery and sixteen serving life sentences for rape.

Less serious offences may be dealt with under a variety of
Acts concerning public order. Rooth (1970) states that in the
past twenty years, there have never been less than 2,000 convictions for indecent exposure per year in England and Wales, and
2,887 convictions were recorded in 1968. In England, the ancient common law left many acts unpunishable which were subse-

quently converted into offences by the Star Chamber and later by the Court of King's Bench, which took over the function of *custos morum* after the restoration of the monarchy. It was this court which made acts of gross public indecency misdemeanours of common law by its judgement of 1663 with the case of Sir Charles Sedley mentioned earlier. English case law provides examples of indecent exposure, some of which, at any rate, one can attribute to exhibitionists: An early case was that mentioned by Judge Park in *R. v. Webb* (1848) 1. Den. 340, who was tried in York in 1830 for exposing to a maid servant from an opposite window. Cases of this kind were arising in increasing numbers from the operation of the revised Vagrancy Act of 1824. The Act recognised three classes of vagrants, of which the main one concerning this subject is that of rogues and vagabonds whose offences might include fortune telling, begging, betting in the street, deserting one's wife and children and "all persons openly exposing in any street, road, public place or highway any indecent exhibition." To this clause the words "or openly and indecently exposing their persons" were added in the final draft. Subsequently, after much debate, a select committee (V. Geo. IV, May 21, 1824) re-introduced the offence, giving it its present form "every person wilfully, openly, ludely and obscenely exposing his person in any street, road or public highway or in view thereof or in every public place of public resort with intent to insult any female." This Bill is still in force.

BIBLIOGRAPHY

Abraham, H. 1956. Contribution to the problem of female sexuality. *Int J Psychoanal, 37,* 351-353.

Bancroft, J. 1969. Aversion therapy of homosexuals. *Br J Psychiatry, 115,* 1417-1431.

Bancroft, J. 1975. *Deviant Sexual Behaviour.* Oxford, Oxford U Pr.

Bancroft, J.H.J., Jones, H.G. and Pullan, B.R. 1966. A simple transducer for measuring penile erection. *Behav Res Ther, 4,* 239.

Belliveau, F. and Richter, L.N. 1970. *Understanding Human Sexual Inadequacy.* London, Hodder and Stroughton; English Universities Press.

Benjamin, H. 1953. Transvestism and transsexualism. *Int J Sexol, 7,* 12-14.

Bentler, P.M. and Prince, C. 1970. Psychiatric symptomatology in transvestites. *J Clin Psychol, 26,* 434-435.

Bieber, I. 1962. *Homosexuality.* New York, Basic.

Bloch, I. 1914. Ein Fall von Exhibitionismus im 16 Jahrhundert. *Z Sexualwissenschaft, 1,* 289-290.

Brecher, R. and Brecher, E. 1965. *Analysis of Human Sexual Response.* New York, NAL.

Bullough, V.L. 1976. *Sexual Variance in Society and History.* New York, Wiley.

Bullough, V.L. 1976. *Psychosexual Problems: Psychotherapy Counselling and Behaviour Modification.* London, Acad Pr; New York, Grune and Stratton.

Burton, K. 1885. *Arabian Nights,* terminal essay. Benares Kamashaskow Soc, Vol. 10, 205-254.

Camps, F.E. 1968. *Gradwohl's Legal Medicine.* Bristol, John Wright & Sons, Ltd.

Cohen, A.D. and Schapiro, A. 1970. Vaginal blood flow during sleep. *Psychophysiology, 7,* 338.

Cooper, A.J. 1969a. An innovation in behavioural treatment of a case of non-consummation due to vaginismus. *Br J Psychiatry, 115,* 721-722.

Cooper, A.J. 1969b. Disorders of sexual potency in the male: A clinical and statistical study of some factors related to short-term prognosis. *Br J Psychiatry, 115,* 709-719.

Cooper, A.J. 1969c. Factors in male sexual inadequacy. A review. *J Nerv Ment Dis, 149,* 337-359.

Cooper, A.J. 1969d. Some personality factors in frigidity. *J Psychosm Res, 13,* 149-155.

Cooper, A.J. 1970. Frigidity. Treatment and short-term prognosis. *J Psychosom Res, 14,* 133-147.

Crown, S. 1976. *Psychosexual Problems: Counselling Psychotherapy and Behavioural Modification.* New York, Acad Pr.

Davis, K.B. 1929. *Factors in the Sex Life of 2,200 Women.* New York, Harper & Brothers.

Deleuze, G. 1971. *Sacher-Masoch: An Interpretation.* London, Faber & Faber.

Dengrove, E. 1967. Behaviour therapy of sexual disorders. *J Sex Research, 3, No. 1,* 49-61.

Dewhurst, K. 1969. Sexual activity and urinary steroids in men with special reference to male homosexuality. *Br J Psychiatry, 115,* 1413-1415.

Dickinson, R.L. and Beam, L. 1931. *A Thousand Marriages.* Baltimore, Williams & Wilkins.

Dorkins, S. and Taylor, R. 1961. Non-consummation of marriage. A survey of 70 cases. *Lancet, 2,* 1029-1032.

Dunn, C.W. 1940. Stilboestrol, induced gynaecomastia in the male. *JAMA, 115,* 2263.

Egerton, J. 1973. The catamites of Boogie Street. *World Medicine,* December 5.

Ellis, A. 1961. *The Art and Practice of Love.* London, Souvenir Press.

Ellis, H. 1928. *Studies in the Psychology of Sex.* Philadelphia, Davis Co., vols. 1-8.

Ellis, H. 1936. Eonism and other studies. In *Studies in the Psychology of Sex.* New York, Random, vol. 2.

Ellison, C. 1968. Psycho-somatic factors in unconsummated marriage. *J Psychosom Res, 12,* 61-65.

Faulk, M. 1971. Factors in the treatment of frigidity. *Br J Psychiatry, 119,* 53-56.

Fenichel, O. 1945. The psychoanalytic theory of neviosis. Norton. New York.

Field, L.H. and Williams, M. 1970. The hormonal treatment of sex offenders. *Med Sci Law, 10,* 27-34.

Freedman, L.A.L.J. 1962. *Virgin Wives.* London, Tavistock.

Freud, S. 1905. Three essays on the theory of sexuality. In *Complete Psychological Works,* Standard Edition. London, vol. 7.

Gadpaille, W.J. 1972. Research into the physiology of maleness and femaleness. *Arch Gen Psychiatry, 26,* 193-206.

Gibbens, T.C.N. and J. Prince. 1963. *Child Victims of Sex Offenses.* London, ISTU.

Gillan, P. 1977. *Sex Therapy Today.* London, Open Books.

Greenacres, P. 1968. Perversions. *Psychoanal Study Child, 23,* 47-62.

Gromske, J. et al. 1969. A case of necrophilia committed in a state of pathological intoxication. *Psychiatr Pol, 3,* 207-209.

Halverson, H.M. 1940. Genital and sphincter behaviour of the male infant. *J Genet Psychol, 56,* 95.

Hamilton, D.M. 1939. Some aspects of homosexuality in relation to total personality development. *Psychiatr Q, 13,* 229-244.

Harlow, H.F. and Harlow, M.K. 1962. The heterosexual affectional system in monkeys. *Am Psychol, 17,* 1-9.

Harris, G.W. 1964. Sex hormones, brain development and brain function. *Endocrinology, 75,* 627-648.

Haslam, M.T. 1965. Treatment of psychogenic dyspareunia by reciprocal inhibition. *Br J Psychiatry, 111,* 280-282.

Haslam, M.T. 1975. A survey of Psychosexual Clinic referrals in York. In *Psychosexual Disorders 1975 Conference Report.* Easingwold, Yorskhire, England, G.H. Smith and Sons.

Haslam, M.T. 1976. Psychosexual disorders and their treatment. *Curr Med Res Op,* 8/2/74; 1/3/75; 10/3/76.

Haslam, M.T. 1978. *Sexual Disorders.* London, Pitman.

Hastings, D.W. 1967. Can specific training procedures overcome sexual inadequacy? In Brecher, R. and Brecher, E. (Eds.). *Analysis of Human Sexual Response.* New York, NAL.

Hirshfield, M. 1910. *Verkleidungstrieb mit Umfangreichen Casuistichen und Historischen Material.* Leipzig, Max Spohr.

Hoenig, J., Kenner, J., and Youd, A. 1970. Social and economic aspects of transsexualism. *Br J Psychiatry, 117,* 163-172.

Hoopes, J.E. et al. 1968. Considerations regarding sexual re-assignment. *J Nerv Ment Dis, 147,* 510-516.

Hopkins, C. 1782. The history of Pygmalion imitated from the tenth book of Ovid's *Metamorphoses.* In *The History of Love.* London, Caslon and Davenhill, 208.

Hyde, H.M. 1964. *A History of Pornography.* London, Heinemann.

Ismail, A.A.A. and Harkness, R.A. 1967. Urinary testosterone excretion in men in normal and pathological conditions. *Acta Endocrinol (Kbh), 56,* 469-480.

Johnson, J. 1965. Prognosis of disorders of sexual potency in the male. *J Psychosom Res, 9,* 195-200.

Johnson, J. 1973. Psychopathia sexualis. *Br J Psychiatry, 122,* 219-220.

Jones, W.H.S. 1948. *Airs, Waters, Places 1722* (Circa 4th century B.C. Hippocrates). London, Heinemann, vol. 1.

Jovanovic, V.J. 1972. *Sexuelle Reaktionen und Schlafperiodic bei Menschen: Ergebnisser Experimenteller Untersuchungen.* Stuttgart, F.E. Verlag.

Kallman, F.J. 1952. Comparative twin study of genetic aspects of male homosexuality. *J Nerv Ment Dis, 115,* 283-298.

Karacan, I. 1969. A simple and inexpensive transducer for quantitative measurements of penile erection during sleep. *Behav Res Meth Inst, 1,* 251.

Karacan, I., Rosenbloom, A.L. and Williams. R.L. 1976. The clitoral erection cycle during sleep. *Psychophysiology, 7,* 335.

Karacan, I., Williams, R.L., Thornby, J.I. and Salis, P.J. 1975. Sleep related penile tumescence as a function of age. *Am J Psychol, 132,* 9.

Kenyon, F.E. 1968. Studies in female homosexuality. *Br J Psychiatry, 114,* 1337.

Kinsey, A.C., Pomeroy, W.B. and Martin, C.E. 1948. *Sexual Behaviour in the Human Male.* Philadelphia and London, Saunders.

Kinsey, A.C., Pomeroy, W.B., Martin, C.E. and Gebhard, P.H. 1953. *Sexual Behaviour in the Human Female.* Philadelphia and London, Saunders.

Koch, F.C. 1936. The biochemistry and physiological significance of the male sex hormone. *J Urol, 35,* 382-398.

Kollar, E.J., Beckwith, W.C. and Edgerton, R.B. 1968. Sexual behaviour of the ARL colony of chimpanzees. *J Nerv Ment Dis, 147,* 444-459.

Krafft-Ebing, R. von. 1886. *Psychopathia Sexualis.* Stuttgart. English translation, London, 1899.

Kullianmull. 1500. *The Anunga Runga* (or *Kamaledhiplava*). *The Stage of Love (The Boat in the Ocean of Love),* English translation, 1800.

Lang, T. 1940. Studies of genetic determination of homosexuality. *J Nerv Ment Dis, 92,* 55-64.

Lazarus, J. 1963. Treatment of frigidity by systematic desensitisation. *J Nerv Ment Dis, 136,* 272-278.

League of Nations. 1938. *Prostitutes: Their Early Lives.* Geneva.

Licht, H. 1926. *Das Liebensleben Der Griechen.* Dresden. English translation, *Sexual Life in Ancient Greece.* New York, Barnes and Noble, 1952.

Lorenz, K.Z. 1958. The evolution of behaviour. *Sci Am, 199,* 67.

Lukianowicz, N. 1959. Survey of various aspects of transvestism in the light of our present knowledge. *J Nerv Ment Dis, 128.*

Malleson, J. 1942. Vaginismus. Its management and psycho-genesis. *Br Med J, 2,* 213.

Marks, I., Gelder, M. and Bancroft, J. 1970. Sexual deviance two years after electricic aversion. *Br J Psychiatry, 117,* 173-185.

Masson, A. 1935. *Le Travestissement* (Dissertation). Paris, Le François.

Masters, W.H. and Johnson, V.E. 1970. *Human Sexual Response.* Waltham, Massachusetts, Little.

Masters, W.H. and Johnson, V.E. 1970. *Human Sexual Inadequacy.* London, Churchill.

Mead, M. 1939. *From the South Seas: Studies of Adolescence and Sex in Primitive Societies.* New York, Morrow.

Mead, M. 1962. *Male and Female.* Harmondsworth, England, Penguin.

Morris, D. 1968. *Naked Ape: A Zoologist's Study of the Human Animal.* New York, McGraw.

Morris, D. 1969. *The Human Zoo.* London, J. Cape.

Nefzauomi Sheikh. 500. *The Perfumed Garden.* English translation by Sir Richard Burton, 1886. Reprinted in 1963 by Luxor Press, London.

Neumann, F. and Elger, W. 1966. Permanent changes in gonadal function and sexual behaviour as a result of early feminisation of male rats by treatment with an anti-androgenic steroid. *Endokrinologie, 50,* 209-224.

Ohlmeyer, P., Brilmayer, H. and Hüllstrung, H. 1944. Periodische Vorganger im Schlaf. *Pfluegens Arch, 248,* 559.

Ovesey, L. 1954. The homosexual conflict. An adaptational analysis. *Psychiatry, 17,* 243-250.

Ovid. 1782. *The Art of Love.* English translation by Dryden, London, Caslon and Davenhill.

Pauly, I.B. 1965. The current status of the sex change operation. *J Nerv Ment Dis, 147, 5,* 460-469.

Peberdy, G. 1969. Premature ejaculation. *Practitioner, 203,* 683.

Perloff, W.H. 1965. In Mamore, J. (Ed.). *Sexual Inversion.* New York, Basic, 44.

Prince, V. 1971. *How to Be a Woman Though Male.* Los Angeles, Chevalier.

Prince, V. and Bentler, P.M. 1972. A survey of 504 cases of transvestism. *Psychol Rep, 31,* 903.

Randall, J.B. 1959. Transvestism and transsexualism. A study of 50 cases. *Br Med J, 1445,* December 1976.

Rasmussen, W.H. 1955. Experimental homosexual behaviour in male albino rats. *Acta Psychol (Amst), 11,* 303-304.

Rawson, R. and Legeza, C. 1975. *Tao: The Chinese Philosophy of Time and Change.* London, Thames and Hudson.

Raymond, M.J. 1969. Aversion therapy for sexual deviations. *Br J Psychiatry, 115,* 525.

Raynor, D.G. 1966. *A Year Among the Girls.* New York, Lyle Stuart.

Robinson, H.A. 1971. Review of child molestation, alleged rape cases. *Am J Obstet Gynecol, 110,* 405-406.

Roeder, R.D. 1970. Medical World News, 25, September 20.

Rooth, F.G. 1970. Some historical notes on indecent exposure and exhibitionism. *Medico-Legal Journals, 38,* 135-139.

Roth, M. and Ball, J.R.B. 1964. *Psychiatric Aspects of Inter-Sexuality: Inter-Sexuality in Vertebrates Including Man.* London, Armstrong; New York, Marshall.

Rush, B. 1830. *Medical Enquiries and Observations upon the Diseases of the Mind.* Philadelphia, Grigg, 347.

Ryrie, C.G. and Brown, J.C. 1976. Endocrine function in homosexuals. *Br Med J, 4,* 685.

Schapiro, A. and Cohen, H.D. 1965. Use of mercury gauges in human measurement. *Trans NY Acad Sci, 27,* 634.

Schapiro, B. 1943. Premature ejaculation. Review of 1,130 cases. *J Urol, 50,* 374-379.

Scott, J.P. 1958. Critical periods in the development of social behaviour in puppies. *Psychosom Med, 20,* 45-54.

Shove, M.F. 1971. Patterns of masochism. An empirical study. *Br J Med Psychol, 44,* 59-66.

Slater, E. 1962. Birth order and maternal age of homosexuals. *Lancet, 1,* 69-71.

Sprenger, J. and Kramer, H. 1928. *Malleus Maleficarum.* Revised English translation by Summers Montague. London, Pushkin Press.

Stoller, R.J. 1970. Pornography and perversion. *Arch Gen Psychiatry, June 22,* 490-499.

Stoller, R.J. 1971. The term transvestism. *Arch Gen Psychiatry, 2214,* 230-237.

Stone, A. and Levine, L. 1950. Group therapy in sexual maladjustment. *Am J Psychiatry, 107,* 195-202.

Storr, A. 1964. *Sexual Deviation.* Harmondsworth, Middlesex, Penguin Books, Ltd.

Swanson, D.W. 1968. Adult sexual abuse of children. *Dis Nerv Syst, 29,* 677-683.

Tanner, J.M. 1955. *Growth and Adolescence.* Oxford, Blackwell.

Tissot, S.A. 1764. *L'Onanisme: Dissertation sur les Maladies Produits par le Masturbation,* 3rd ed. Lausanne, Marcus Chapius et Cie.

Tucker, E.C. 1971. Clinical evaluation and management of the impotent. *J Am Ger Assoc, 19, 2,* 180-186.

Van de Velde, T.H. 1965. *Ideal Marriage: Its Physiology and Technique.* English translation by S. Browne. New York, Random.

Vatsyayana. 500. *The Kama Sutra.* English translation from the Sanskrit by Sir Richard Burton and F.F. Arbuthnot, 1880. Reprinted in 1963. London, Kimber.

Werner, A.A. 1969. Male climacteric. *JAMA, 112,* 1441-1443.

West, D.J. 1955. *Homosexuality.* Harmondsworth, Middlesex, Penguin Books, Ltd.

West, D.J. 1976. *Homosexuality Re-examined.* London, Duckworth.

Whittaker, L.H. 1959. Oestrogen and psycho-sexual disorders. *Med J Aust, 2,* 347.

Wise, T.A. 1845. *Commentary on the Hindu System of Medicine.* Calcutta, Thacker.

Wong, A.D. and Wu, L.T. 1936. *History of Chinese Medicines.* Shanghai,

National Quarantine Service.

Yaffé, M. and Tennent, T.G.   1973.   Pornography.   A psychological appraisal.   *Br J Hosp Med,* March.

Zavitzianos, G.   1971.   Fetishism and exhibitionism in the female and their relationship to psychopathy and cleptomania.   *Int J Psychoanal, 52,* 297-305.

Zechmeh, R.   1971.   Exhibitionism.   Genesis, dynamics and treatment.   *Psychiatr Q, 45,* 70-75.

INDEX

189